D0910206

PRAISE FROM FAMOUS MEN:
An Anthology of Introductions

Selected and Edited by

GUY R. LYLE

With a Preface on Prefaces by

KEVIN GUINAGH

The Scarecrow Press, Inc.
Metuchen, N.J.   1977

Library of Congress Cataloging in Publication Data
Main entry under title:

Praise from famous men.

    1. Prefaces. I. Lyle, Guy Redvers, 1907-
PN171.P7P67   808.84   76-55402
ISBN 0-8108-1002-6

TO THE READER

Preliminaries fascinate me. They are rooted in our life habits. They are to be observed in the handshake before a baseball or football game, in the clinking of glasses before a toast, in the overture to an opera, in the breaking of a champagne bottle over the prow at ship-launching, in the command for silence at the opening of court, in the presentation of a speaker, and in the introduction to a book. Some years ago my old and dear friend, Kevin Guinagh, who provides an inviting preface on prefaces to the present work, collaborated with me in the compilation of a book entitled, I Am Happy to Present, which had a modest reception and was expanded in a second edition. Praise from Famous Men: An Anthology of Introductions is intended as a companion volume. Both deal with a neglected literary genre which has been edged out of the limelight by the greater variety and volume of other literary forms.

It should not be too difficult to find a unifying force or common mood in making a selection for an anthology of introductions and prefaces by contemporary writers. The glue to bind them together could be the interest in the subject matter itself, the intimate feeling and character of the introductions, or the generosity of those who have arrived reaching down a helping hand to those who are trying to climb. Perhaps each of these has had some influence in my selections, particularly the last named, but the simple truth is that the anthology makes no pretense to a unifying principle. The reader is free to roam as he will, with no great labor of search or expense of time. The introductions are all by gifted men and women and the whole is nicely fitted to John Drinkwater's prescription for "entertainment for serendipity minds at the last half-hour before the light is switched off at night." I have omitted several prefaces which I would have liked to include because the necessary permission was not forthcoming except at an exorbitant charge. On the other hand I am certain there are many interesting and important introductions which I have overlooked because of the limitations of my own reading.

iii

Perhaps the miscellaneous quality of the collection may be excused if it sends the casual reader back to some of the books which are introduced. With this in mind I have added a prefatory note to each selection, in the hope that it says something informative and interesting about the books themselves.

I wish to acknowledge the assistance of the Reference Department staff of the Woodruff Library of Emory University for reference assistance; my friend, Kevin Guinagh, for valuable suggestions and advice; Miss Ruth Walling, Associate University Librarian, Emory University, for research assistance, reading the manuscript, and making helpful suggestions for improvement; and my wife, Margaret, for criticism, correction, and typing.

G. R. L.

May 1976

CONTENTS

v

A PREFACE ON PREFACES

In the first pages of his book an author tries to tell the reader why he should read his work. He naturally hopes it will enjoy a wide distribution and with that end in view, he indicates the purpose he had in writing it and the need for such a study. In an introduction he may outline the contents of the text and ease the reader into the subject. He makes a respectful bow to other investigations but lets it be known that he is giving the public new material, even slyly suggesting that he has extended the frontiers of learning. Authors are not a modest tribe, and some may suggest the excellence of their product to a degree that many may judge boastful. George Bernard Shaw's prefaces, collected in a thick volume, are not notable for their modesty; but then he had trained Shavians to accept his excessive self-esteem.

These first pages are often called a preface, a word English has taken directly from French, which took it from the Latin praefatio. A surprising number of other terms have been employed as a caption for this prefatory material. Sometimes foreword is used. This is an English translation of preface and literally means something that is said before something else. Caxton, the father of English printing, called the preface a prologue, the equivalent of preface but derived from the Greek. He published nearly a hundred books, and their prologues, unhurried, charming and sometimes rambling, have been collected in a single volume.

Other captions have been used by the learned for prefatory material: proem from the Latin procemium meaning introduction, prolegomena from the Greek for matters that are treated beforehand, and preamble--found in legal documents.

Sometimes this section of a book may take the form of a dedication. Today this is a brief expression of love or esteem for a person close to the author or even unknown to him but held in admiration because of the example or inspiration he furnished the author. At times a work is dedicated to

persons indicated only by initials or first names, a practice
suggesting this is a very private matter. These secretive
expressions of affection stand in sharp contrast to the ful-
some dedications of former days when in the most flowery
language writers courted the favor of powerful statesmen or
clergymen in the hope of gaining largess or protection. Often
these exercises in flattery described with resounding superla-
tives the nobility, generosity and other assorted virtues of a
patron. The extreme is found in the dedication of Robert
Herrick's Hesperides and Noble Numbers: "To the Most Illustrious, and Most Hopefull Prince Charles, Prince of
Wales ... my Works creator, and alone / The Flame of it,
and the Expansion. / And look how all those heavenly lamps
acquire / Light from the Sun, that inexhausted Fire. / So
all my Morne, and Evening Stars from You / Have their Existence, and their Influence too."

However, some of the great prefaces in the form of
dedications were written with restraint, though the motive
was still clear. When John Calvin dedicated his Institutes of
the Christian Religion to Francis I, he was seeking protection
from physical harm for his followers and consideration for
his religious doctrine. Here there is no flattery of the
French King, in contrast to Herrick's praise of Charles. It
was a shrewd move by no means sycophantic on the part of
Copernicus to dedicate his work On the Revolutions of the
Heavenly Bodies to Pope Paul III. Without the protection of
His Holiness, critics tied to the traditional cosmology would
have made the scientist's life miserable just as they did
Galileo's almost a century later. There was no gross flat-
tery in Erasmus' dedication of his Praise of Folly to Sir
Thomas More, a few playful pages by a brilliant humanist to
a witty lawyer.

In the eighteenth century the word advertisement was
used for what we call a preface. When we think of an advertisement, we feel that somebody is attempting to sell us
something. This commercial motive was not entirely foreign
to those authors who introduced their works in this fashion.
Boswell used it as a preface to his Life of Johnson in an effort to promote his book. He added a flattering dedication
to Sir Joshua Reynolds, whose name he felt would lend the
work prestige. In Lyrical Ballads Wordsworth stated in his
"advertisement" that the poems were "written chiefly with
a view to ascertain how far the language of conversation in
the middle and lower classes is adapted to the purposes of

poetic pleasure." In a polite way he was canvassing the possibility of a new market for poetry.

A preface will generally list a series of acknowledgments, an important section from the author's point of view. He may express his appreciation to those who inspired his work or who read his manuscript and caught several errors, though he is careful to point out that he alone is responsible for any mistakes that may be found in the text. A reader interested in the accuracy or credibility of a work and who is himself competent in the area treated will scan the list for the names of those who read the manuscript, for it is assumed that no scholar of standing would risk tarnishing his reputation by approving a book that might later be attacked by just criticism.

An author or compiler of a book is careful to indicate his appreciation of the publishers who have permitted him to quote from their publications, though convention opposes his mentioning the fee he had to pay for the privilege, sometimes excessive. However, the copyright owner has a right to control his material and when permission to quote is granted and not acknowledged, the omission can be costly. A late friend reproduced material in one of her books gratis under the strict proviso that certain exact wording was to be used or there would be a charge of five hundred dollars. Through some bungling the phrasing was not printed as ordered by the copyright owner. The fee was demanded and my friend paid.

Sometimes the list of those to whom the author is grateful is long, frequently ending with a touching tribute to the devotion of a spouse without whose inspiration, help and encouragement the work would not have been attempted or completed. This is no perfunctory compliment. No matter how devout such a decoration, it does scant credit to the labor of typing the manuscript, reading proofs, checking sources and preparing an index, all boring but exacting and important chores. Finally there may be a modest suggestion that the author welcomes word of any errors readers may find in his book.

No matter by what name the preface is called--foreword, introduction, prologue, proem, prolegomena, dedication or advertisement--it is aimed at public interest with the hope that the distribution of the work may be increased.

PREFACE ON PREFACES

The preface has deep roots in literary history. Livy (59 B. C. -A. D. 17) opens his history of Rome with a formal preface in a fine piece of Latin. He wonders if he is making good use of his time, seeing that the subject has been treated before by many authors. However, he takes satisfaction in the thought that he will be chronicling the achievements of the greatest people in the world. Should his work be ignored by posterity, he knows his fame will be eclipsed by illustrious historians who have written before him. He prefers to narrate the early history of Rome rather than discuss the great evils of his own day, riddled with avarice and luxury. By examining the lives of virtuous and evil men, the readers of his history would find heroic models to imitate. In his mind this was the only valid reason for recording historical events.

Before the actual text on the conspiracy of Catiline, Sallust writes a preface in which he discusses the superiority of mental power over the merely physical. He admits that in his youth he was caught up in the pursuit of an unworthy fame, but he is happy that in his later years he returned to the studies of his earlier days and devoted himself to the writing of history. The poet Martial wrote a preface in prose to defend himself against the critics of his epigrams, at the same time venting his anger against plagiarists who worked over his material and took the credit for themselves. The preface, then, is not a modern invention.

In the Middle Ages most writing was done by clerics. Their manuscripts were often unsigned. Since much of what was written in those days concerned doctrines of the Church, there was little room for sweeping originality. The ideal of the monastic life was personal anonymity; individual advancement by literary achievement was not encouraged by the hierarchy. This is one reason why questions arose after the invention of the printing press over the authorship of works that had long circulated in manuscript. In works printed in the fifteenth century we find personal prefaces by the great editors like Aldus Manutius.

The hasty reader goaded by academic compulsion to digest a book or deeply interested in the subject itself may ignore the prefatory section, regarding it as the private concern of the author and publisher. He moistens his forefinger and flips over these first pages. In his haste he is often passing over very important material. Notable essays in English literature have appeared as prefaces. The list is

PREFACE ON PREFACES

long and it includes the introductions to Spenser's Faerie Queene, Dryden's Fables, Johnson's Shakespeare, Wordsworth's Lyrical Ballads, and Whitman's Leaves of Grass, to name a few. Such prefaces as these must have been in Christopher Morley's thoughts when he wrote in a moment of enthusiasm, "Better a preface than a book," one of those pleasantly outrageous exaggerations designed to stress a point and call attention to a thing of value.

Some readers are prejudiced against prefaces and readily confess that on opening a book they immediately turn to the first chapter. With them, passing over the preface is a habit, a matter of policy. They are not necessarily students of the modern school of rapid readers who take lessons on how to read a page at a glance; they may read for pleasure and slowly savor the taste of good writing. Ignoring the preface of a book, they may miss some very interesting reading, such as E. B. White's preface to A Sub-Treasury of American Humor or G. K. Chesterton's commendation of Fulton Sheen's God and Intelligence, the first book of about fifty that he would later write, or Will Durant's remarks at the beginning of each of the eleven volumes of his History of Civilization, in which he questions from volume to volume the possibility of living long enough to finish his panorama of man's inheritance, comparing himself to the prima donna who makes one last concert tour several times.

An author does not write the preface before he writes his book. This he composes at the end of the battle in which he has forced his resisting ideas onto paper. It is often a paean of victory, a moment of rejoicing, of looking back over a long period of frustration and self-denial. He may be compared to a lecturer, highly stimulated after his performance, who steps down from the podium and seeks a rendezvous where he chats intimately with his friends. It is here that one may often catch a glimpse of the kind of person the author really is and learn something of his work, his problems and personal characteristics. What a mistake it would be to avoid Samuel Johnson's preface to his dictionary of the English language. Here he reveals much of a personality that has engaged the attention of readers since Boswell gave us this literary dictator's biography. He was certainly in one of his depressed moods when he began his essay by stating that those who toil at the lower levels of life are driven by the fear of evil rather than the prospect of good. "Among these unhappy mortals is the writer of dictionaries.... Every other author may aspire to praise; the lexicographer can only hope to escape reproach." However, he expresses satisfaction at the thought of his accomplishment. "I have devoted this book, the labor of years, to the honor of my country." He holds that the chief glory of a people arises from its authors. On his own literary survival he dares not speculate; he offers excuses for what he regarded as his limited body of literary accomplishments: the pressure of diseases, the frittering away of time and the problem of providing for the needs of the moment. He ends his essay on a sad note: "I have protracted my work till most of those whom I wished to please have sunk into the grave, and success and miscarriage are empty sounds: I therefore dismiss it with frigid tranquility, having little to fear or hope from censure or from praise."

Generally the author of a book writes his own preface. Sometimes a person with a magic name in literary circles may be asked to write an introduction for a newcomer to the world of publishing. This task a writer of reputation will consider with great deliberation, realizing that if the work is inferior, his judgment will be criticized and reputation harmed in consequence. However, at times a noted writer will introduce to the reading world a talent he has discovered. In a few enthusiastic pages he may raise a work into the light of prominence. In so doing he becomes a kind of patron, a Maecenas reaching out to help a Horace or a Vergil. Surely next in fame to writing a work of solid merit is discovering a previously unknown or unrecognized talent and introducing him to an audience predisposed to be friendly by reason of the commendation of a respected judge. This joy of discovery must be the source of great personal satisfaction and may be compared to the thrill a miner must feel when after panning for gold all his life, he suddenly finds a nugget.

In the following pages Mr. Lyle has given us a series of prefaces in which distinguished persons commend a work they hold in high regard and which they feel is worthy of wide recognition. In doing so they have been generous and unselfish, hoping to persuade their own audience to read what they regard so highly. This is the kind of patron every author hopes to find, a person of reputation who admires his literary efforts and strives to win others over to share his enthusiasm.

KEVIN GUINAGH

W. H. AUDEN

The Art of Eating is the kind of cookery book that plain cooks are not going to like. It turns upon personality, it contains scores of complicated recipes from hot winter borscht to a savorous concoction called "Hang Two Fry," and it dips and wanders into a variety of side roads describing the love-life of the oyster and other fascinating facts of natural history, as well as anecdotes gleaned from Larousse, Brillat-Savarin, and other French gastronomical works. But the plain cooks will for the most part be wrong. The Art of Eating is no recipe book, although it contains many mouth-watering, albeit extravagant recipes. It is half-culinary and half-literary and it is written by a woman of a definite and likeable personality who has led a varied life, lived in many places, and known many interesting people.

In a performance of considerable charm, well suited to the book and the warm reality of the author's personality, the poet W. H. Auden provides a foreword to The Art of Eating in which he writes that Mrs. Fisher has met three tests in the art and appreciation of good cooking. She is "a practicing cook, not a member of some Wine and Food Society"; cooking is her avocation, not her profession: "She knows her guests as friends, lovers, husbands, so that she is able to relate their gastronomical habits to the rest of their personalities"; and thirdly, she has the sophistication to write simply and well. It is "a book," he adds, "for the library rather than the kitchen shelf." It might also be mentioned that Mrs. Fisher is a gastronomic scholar. The magnum opus in the gastronomic art is Brillat-Savarin's witty treatise on the art of dining, which Mrs. Fisher has translated into English under the title The Physiology

1

of Taste. It may be an exaggeration when Auden
writes "I do not know of anyone in the United States
today who writes better prose," but undoubtedly Mrs.
Fisher's original work gives her high ranking among
essayists as well as social historians. The Art of
Eating should be in every mother's lap--and father's,
too.

INTRODUCTION BY W. H. AUDEN

to M. F. K. Fisher's
The Art of Eating

    Though it contains a number of recipes, The Art of
Eating is a book for the library rather than the kitchen shelf.
If it were simply a manual of culinary technique, I could not
discuss it because, much as I enjoy reading recipes, they
remain for me mysterious magical spells; like most people
who cannot cook, I cannot combine the various ingredients in
my imagination so as to guess what the dish will taste like.
When, for example, I read Mrs. Fisher's recipe for Prune
Roast, though I have no doubt that it is delicious, I can only
taste the prunes in isolation and shudder.

    For the benefit of readers who are also cooks and
therefore in a position to judge, I asked a friend upon whose
authority I rely to select three recipes as examples of her
taste and skill. He chose Hot Winter Borscht, Hindu Eggs
1949 and Hamburgers à la Mode de Moi-même. All three
are simple well-known dishes. A comparison of her versions
with what is generally served demonstrates the truth of Count-
ess Morphy's dictum: "Plain cooking cannot be entrusted to
plain cooks. "

    Cooking is an art and its appreciation, therefore, is
governed by the law which applies to all artistic appreciation.
Those who have been subjected too long and too exclusively
to bad cooking become incapable of recognizing good cooking
if and when they encounter it. Nobody can afford to keep a
good professional cook any more and, though there are still
good restaurants, their prices are geared to people with expense accounts. For most of us, the possibility of eating
well depends upon the skill and passion of the amateur cook,
and learning the art should now be regarded as essential to

an educated man or woman. At Oxford and Cambridge, for example, I should like to see a stove installed in every under-graduate's room and the College dining-halls transformed into supermarkets and liquor-stores. In the meantime, I would recommend all parents (and godparents) to present their children of both sexes on their sixteenth birthday with a copy of The Art of Eating. It will not teach them how to cook, but I cannot think of any other reading-matter which is more likely to inspire them with the desire to learn.

The Art of Eating is about Food and People. For such a theme Mrs. Fisher is singularly well qualified. In the first place, cooking is her avocation not her profession. Several famous chefs have published their reminiscences but, in describing their clients, they are at the disadvantage of having only known them as diners, but Mrs. Fisher has also known her guests as friends, lovers, husbands, so that she is able to relate their gastronomical habits to the rest of their personalities. Again, since she is not a professional tied to a kitchen, she is free to dine in restaurants and at the tables of others and is immune from professional jealousy.

In the second place, though she is an amateur by sta-tus, she is a practicing cook, not a member of some Wine and Food Society. The difference between an expert cook and a professional gourmet is the difference between an artist and a connoisseur: because he does not work for his pleasure but only pays for it, the connoisseur can, and only too often does, divorce pleasure from love. There is a kind of gour-met who writes about eating in the same way that an elderly roué talks about sex and the effect on me is the same--he makes all pleasure sound disgusting: after listening to him holding forth about some exquisite meal he had in 1910, I feel like living on capsules for the rest of my life.

Last but not least, Mrs. Fisher is as talented a writ-er as she is a cook. Indeed, I do not know of anyone in the United States today who writes better prose. If a reader wishes to test this assertion, let him turn to the first three pages of the section in "An Alphabet for Gourmets" entitled "I is for Innocence."

It is extraordinary how little attention has been paid by either historians or novelists to the eating habits of na-tions, generations and individuals. Nobody, so far as I know has seriously tackled the history of cooking, which is full of

fascinating problems.   For instance, neither the potato nor
pasta were native to Europe and must, when first introduced,
have been exotic foods.   How did they become staple diets?
Why did the northern peoples take to the potato and the Ital-
ians to pasta?   Today, when no nation can live in isolation
and mass travel has become possible, such questions have
assumed great political importance.   The average man is
more conservative in his gastronomical habits than in any
others; at the same time, the greatest insult one can offer
to another is to refuse the food he provides.   Americans intending to travel abroad now receive a letter from the President reminding them that, even as tourists, they are emis-
saries of their country.   Food, I am sorry to say, is not
mentioned.   Every tourist ought to be warned that, if he re-
fuses to eat the typical food of the country he is visiting,
he is doing more to create ill will than if he stole it.

Such adaptation is, of course, not always easy.   "What
is patriotism," wrote Lin Yutang, "but the love of the good
things we ate in our childhood?"   But it is also true that one
reason why we find certain dishes good is because we ate
them in childhood.   Having grown up in England, I belong to
a class of persons for whom Mrs. Fisher feels an exas-
perated pity, those who desire potatoes twice a day.   When
I started to read her description of The Perfect Dinner, my
mouth watered but, presently, I came to the main meat
course with which she serves noodles and I salivated no more.
I can eat noodles or spaghetti or even rice, but they say
nothing to me, whereas I can hear a song in any overboiled
elderly spud.   There are certain tastes which those who have
never experienced them as children can neither understand
nor cure: who but an Englishman, for example, can know the
delights of stone-cold leathery toast for breakfast, or the
wonders of Dead Man's Leg?

It is no accident that the central rite of the Christian
religion, its symbol for agape, love untainted by selfish desire or self-projection, should be the act of eating bread and
drinking wine.   For such a symbol, a sexual rite would never do.   In the first place, since it presupposes two different
sexes, it divides as well as unites; in the second, it is not
intrinsically selfish enough.   Though it is necessary to the
survival of the race, the sexual act is not necessary to the
survival of the individual so that, even at its crudest, it
contains an element of giving.   Eating, on the other hand is

4

a pure act of taking. Only the absolutely necessary and absolutely self-regarding can stand as a symbol for its opposite, the absolutely voluntary and self-forgetful. From watching the way in which a person eats, one can learn a great deal about the way in which he loves himself and, consequently, about the way he will probably love or hate his neighbor. The behavior towards others of the gobbler will be different from that of the pecker, of the person who eats his titbit first from the person who leaves his to the last.

Mrs. Fisher gives us a whole gallery of portraits. Here, for example, is Madame Biarnet.

> She ate like a madwoman, crumbs falling from her mouth, her cheeks bulging, her eyes glistening and darting about the plates and cups and her hands tearing at chunks of meat and crusts of bread. Occasionally she stopped long enough to put a tiny bite between the wet delicate lips of her little terrier Tango, who sat silently on her knees through every meal. . . . She drank only in Lent, for some deeply hidden reason. Then she grew uproarious and affectionate and finally tearful on hot spiced Moulin à Vent in which she sopped fried pastries called Friandaises de Carême. They immediately became very limp and noisy to eat, and she loved them; a way to make long soughings which irritated her husband and satisfied her bitter insistence that we are all beasts.

And here is a horrible young American blonde.

> She smoked all through the meal, which none of us was doing, and once, when she let her pretty arm fall towards Chexbres and the fingers unfold commandingly, I saw him pick up the cigarette box and offer it to her, so that she had to lift her hand again and choose one for herself, and I knew that he was deeply angry with her, in spite of his wisdom and tolerance.
> The rest of us were disjointing our little brown birds and eating them in our fingers, as is only proper on a summer night among friends in a friendly room. But the girl cut one little piece off one side of the breast, one little piece off the other, and then pushed the plump carcase almost fretfully away. She

picked a few late summer peas from the vegetables
on her plate, and ate a little bread, and then asked
Chexbres for coffee.

The portrait which Mrs. Fisher draws of herself interests
me very much.   On her own showing, she believes in and
practices equality of the sexes: there is nothing of the Little Woman about her.   The male wolf neither frightens nor
shocks her--she sounds as if she were quite capable of
playing the wolf herself--she knows how to handle waiters
and can dine alone in a restaurant with perfect composure.

If this self-portrait is accurate, it confirms a theory
of mine that in most women who develop a passion for cooking, their animus, their unconscious masculine side, is unusually strong, while in men who show the same passion,
it is their anima which is stronger than normal.   One might
put it like this.   The male who loves cooking as an art
owes this love to the fact that he has no breasts; in his female colleague, the origin of such a love is the wish that
her status as a human person shall not depend upon her possessing them.   (I wish some psychologist would provide a
convincing explanation of why murder is commoner among
cooks than among the members of any other profession.)

By social custom, in all households except those rich
enough to afford a professional chef, it is the woman not the
man who does the cooking, but there is no reason to suppose that an avocation for cooking is commoner among women
than among men.   One can generally spot the woman who
does not love cooking for its own sake by two symptoms.
If she is cooking for somebody she likes, she may cook
very well but she almost always serves too much; if, on
the other hand, she dislikes or is angry with the person
she is obliged to feed, no matter how good a cook she can
be, she almost always cooks badly.   Men are not socially
obliged to cook, so that a man for whom cooking is not a
passion seldom prepares a meal except for a girl he is trying to make.   His characteristic culinary defect is due to
the self-centeredness of the masculine imagination; he tends
to plan his meal in terms of what he imagines would seduce
him if he were a woman.

Mrs. Fisher has attended a number of such Bachelor
Dinners and has some shrewd observations to make.

I have found that most bachelors like the exotic, at least, culinarily speaking: they would rather fuss around with a complex recipe for Le Hochepot de Queue de Bœuf than a simple one called Stewed Ox-tail, even if both come from Andre Simon's <u>Concise Encyclopedia of Gastronomy</u>.... The drink is good. He pops discretely in and out of his gastronomical workshop, where he brews his sly receipts, his digestive attacks upon the fortress of her virtue. She represses her natural curiosity, and if she is at all experienced in such wars, she knows fairly well that she will have a patterned meal which has already been indicated by his ordering in restaurants. More often than not it will be some kind of chicken, elaborately disguised with everything from Australian pine-nuts to herbs grown by the landlady's daughter.

In the reverse situation when it is the Spinster--or shall we say the Merry Widow?--who is giving the dinner, men are so transparent that she can hardly go wrong. If he is shy, the right kind and right amount of alcohol may be important, but the food is unlikely to affect his intentions. The only mistake she can make is to serve her Desirable Guest with some dish to which he happens to have a profound aversion, rooted in childhood. No matter how charming the server, I should have to be very much in love indeed to survive Cold Shape or Sago Pudding. But, being a woman, this is a mistake the Merry Widow scarcely ever makes. Her problem is more likely to be one of trying to avoid having to say No and thus spoiling a pleasant evening. If she can cook, she has only to follow Mrs. Fisher's recipe, which is guaranteed to reduce the most ardent wooer to a clumbering mass of masculine inactivity.

> I would serve one too many Martinis, that is, about three. Then while his appetite raged, thus whipped with alcohol, I would serve generous, rich, salty Italian hors d'œuvres: prosciutto, little chilled marinated shrimps, olives stuffed with anchovy, spiced and pickled tomatoes--things that would lead him on. Next would come something he no longer wanted but couldn't resist, something like a ragout of venison, or squabs stuffed with mushrooms and wild rice, and plenty of red wine, sure danger after the cocktails and the highly salted appetisers. I

would waste no time on a salad, unless perhaps a
freakish rich one, treacherously containing truffles and
new potatoes.   The dessert would be cold, superficial-
ly refreshing and tempting, but venomous; a chilled
bowl of figs soaked in kirsch with heavy cream.
There would be a small bottle of Sauterne, sly and
icy, or a judicious bit of champagne, and then a
small cup of coffee so black and bitter that my victim could not down it, even therapeutically.

On every social aspect of eating, beginning with the gastronomic education of children, Mrs. Fisher shows wisdom and
common sense.

Gastronomical perfection can be reached in these com-
binations: one person dining alone, usually upon a
couch or a hillside; two persons, of no matter what
sex or age, dining in a good restaurant; six people
of no matter what sex or age, dining in a good
home.... A good combination would be one married
couple, for warm composure; one less firmly established, to add a note of interrogation to the talk; and
two strangers of either sex, upon whom the better ac-
quainted could sharpen their questioning wits.

Only on the subject of the Family dinner do I find her
shocking.   However psychologically beneficial it may prove
to shift Father's position at table and serve untraditional
food, it still seems to me blasphemous.   What is the use
of pretending one can treat the members of one's own family
as ordinary human beings?

As an observer of the human condition, Mrs. Fisher
has led a varied life.   She came from what must have been
a happy family and has children of her own.   She has lived
in many places, Alsace, Dijon, Switzerland, Italy, Mexico,
and met all kinds of persons from peasants to Hollywood
film-stars.   She has lived in boardinghouses, rented apart-
ments and homes.   She has known poverty and relative af-
fluence.   She has had several husbands, with one of whom
she had to live in the knowledge that he was doomed to die
presently from an incurable disease.

Of her many stories and anecdotes, some are hilari-
ous, some macabre, some tragic.   If most of them are bit-

ter-sweet, she is never saccharine nor acid. The Art of
Eating is a book which I think Colette would have loved and
wished she had written.

STANLEY BALDWIN

It was in Shropshire County, in the west part of England, that Mary Webb spent her childhood and her comparatively brief adulthood. She was born March 25, 1881, struggled all her life against crushing poverty and ill-health, and died at the early age of forty-six. Yet in her brief lifetime, burdened though it was by the necessity of doing a laborer's work to eke out a living for her family, she found time to write six novels and a volume of poems and essays. All these writings suffered the same indifference the world had shown to their author. Sir James Barrie spoke of her as "the best of our writers, yet no one buys her books." Even the Times Literary Supplement, during her lifetime at least, paid little attention to her writings.

It was quite by chance that Stanley Baldwin, then prime minister of Great Britain, was given a copy of Precious Bane by one of his secretaries just as he was about to leave on a vacation. This novel, published some three years before her death, had its setting in her native Shropshire with which Baldwin was very familiar. Mary Webb knew the folkways, knew the legends and old stories; and in her writings showed an extraordinary delicacy of sensibility to nature and to natural life. Baldwin was so moved by the book's lyrical beauty and compassion that on his return he wrote Mary Webb a personal letter of warm encouragement. His introduction to Precious Bane, which did not appear until after her death, aroused such widespread interest in the author and her books that she became a best-seller.

STANLEY BALDWIN

INTRODUCTION BY STANLEY BALDWIN

to Mary Webb's
Precious Bane

Mary Meredith, the author of Precious Bane, was
born in the little village of Leighton, near Cressage, under
the Wrekin, on March 25th, 1881, and died at St. Leonards,
October 8th, 1927, and was buried at Shrewsbury. She was
the daughter of George Edward Meredith, a schoolmaster of
Welsh descent, by his marriage with Sarah Alice Scott,
daughter of an Edinburgh doctor of the clan of Sir Walter
Scott. She was the eldest of six children and spent her
early girlhood at The Grange, a small country house near
Much Wenlock; from 12 to 21 she lived at Stanton-on-Hine-
Heath, six miles northeast of Shrewsbury, and for the next
ten years at The Old Mill, Meole Brace, a mile from
Shrewsbury. In 1912 Mary Meredith married Mr. Henry
Bertram Law Webb, a Cambridge graduate and a native of
Shropshire. After two years at Weston-super-Mare, where
Mr. Webb had a post in a school, Mr. and Mrs. Webb returned to Shropshire, living at Pontesbury and Lyth Hill,
working as market gardeners and selling the produce at their
own stall in Shrewsbury market. Mrs. Webb had written
stories and poems from childhood, but it was at this period
that she seriously turned her mind to writing novels. A
volume of essays on nature, The Spring of Joy, and three
novels, The Golden Arrow, Gone to Earth, and The House
in Dormer Forest, had been published before she came to live
in London in 1921. Seven for a Secret followed in 1922 and
Precious Bane in 1924. It was awarded the "Femina Vie
Heureuse" Prize for 1924-5 given annually for the best work
of imagination in prose or verse descriptive of English life
by an author who had not attained sufficient recognition.

I am indebted for these biographical particulars to Mr.
Webb to whom Precious Bane is inscribed. I never met
Mary Webb and knew nothing of her work until I read Precious Bane at Christmas, 1926. I am glad to think that I
was in time to send her a few words of appreciation.

The stupid urban view of the countryside as dull re-
ceives a fresh and crushing answer in the books of Mary

11

Webb. All the novels except <u>Precious Bane</u> are set in the
hill country of south-west Shropshire, between the Clee Hills
and the Breiddens, and between Shrewsbury and Ludlow.
The scene of <u>Precious Bane</u> is the country of north Shropshire meres--the <u>Ellesmere</u> district, but the dialect is that
of south Shropshire.   It is the country of the Severn low-
lands and of isolated upland ridges where Celt and Saxon have
met and mingled for centuries.   For the passing traveller it
is inhabited by an uncommunicative population dwelling among
places with names like Stedment and Squilver and Stiperstone,
Nipstone and Nind.   There are of course the old castles and
timbered black and white houses for the motoring visitors.
But to the imaginative child brought up among the ploughlands
and pools and dragonflies there is "a richness on the world,
so it looked what our parson used to call sumptuous." It is
this richness which Mary Webb saw and felt as a girl and
remembered with lyrical intensity as a woman.

She has interlaced with this natural beauty the tragic
drama of a youth whose whole being is bent on toil and thrift
and worldly success only to find himself defeated on the mor-
row of the harvest by the firing of the cornricks by the father
of his lover.   The dour figure of Gideon Sarn is set against
that of his gentle sister, Prudence, who tells the tale.   She
is a woman flawed with a hare-shotten lip and cursed in the
eyes of the neighbours until her soul's loveliness is discerned
by Kester Woodseaves, the weaver.   And so there comes to
her at the end of the story the love which is "the peace to
which all hearts do strive."

The strength of the book is not in its insight into human character, though that is not lacking.   Nor does it lie
in the inevitability with which the drama is unfolded and the
sin of an all-absorbing and selfish ambition punished.   It
lies in the fusion of the elements of nature and man, as observed in this remote countryside by a woman even more
alive to the changing moods of nature than of man.   Almost
any page at random will furnish an illustration of the blend-
ing of human passion with the fields and skies.

> So they rode away, and the sound of the people died
> till it was less than the hum of a midge, and there
> was nothing but a scent of rosemary, and warm sun,
> and the horse lengthening its stride towards the moun-
> tains, whence came the air of morning [p. 117].

STANLEY BALDWIN

One reviewer compared <u>Precious Bane</u> to a sampler stitched through long summer evenings in the bay window of a remote farmhouse. And sometimes writers of Welsh and Border origin, like William Morris, have had their work compared to old tapestries. But while these comparisons suggest something of the harmonies of colour they fail to convey the emotional force which glows in these pages. Nature to Mary Webb was not a pattern on a screen. Her sensibility is so acute and her power over words so sure and swift that one who reads some passages in Whitehall has almost the physical sense of being in Shropshire cornfields.

<u>Precious Bane</u> is a revelation not of unearthly but of earthly beauty in one bit of the England of Waterloo, the Western edge, haunted with the shadows of superstition, the legendary lore and phantasy of neighbours on the Border, differing in blood and tongue. This mingling of peoples and traditions and turns of speech and proverbial wisdom is what Mary Webb saw with the eye of the mind as she stood at her stall in Shrewsbury market, fastened in her memory, and fashioned for us in the little parcel of novels which is her legacy to literature.

STANLEY BALDWIN

10 Downing Street, S. W. 1.
October, 1928

JAMES M. BARRIE

Described by his first publisher as a "dark, Semitic, sensitive type," Leonard Merrick--he was Leonard Miller by birth and took the name of Merrick for acting purposes--was born in London, February 21, 1864. Intended for the bar, he went to private school and Brighton College but his father's financial reverses prevented him from completing his studies. At age eighteen he left England and found work as a foreman of black laborers in the diamond fields of South Africa. A few years later he returned home, joined an acting company in London, and toured England with a sensational Drury Lane melodrama. At this time he adopted the stage name Merrick which he later acquired legally.

Early disappointed in his hopes as an actor, Merrick took up writing, but for a considerable time had little success. Discouraged by his reception in London he borrowed money to go to the United States, which proved equally disappointing, both in his efforts to get a part in a play and to find a publisher for his manuscripts. Returning home, he resumed the struggle to become a writer, in Paris as well as in London. In 1918, after the publication of his twelfth novel, a group of well-known authors and friends arranged the publication of an appreciative edition of his works, an unusual honor for any living author and particularly for one who had failed to secure a wide reading public. Each of the novels in this edition was prefaced by one of his fellow-authors. The praise of these men, including such distinguished writers as Sir James Barrie, Sir Arthur Pinero, William J. Locke, G.

14

JAMES M. BARRIE

K. Chesterton, and H. G. Wells, eventually assured
him of success.
In the introduction to Merrick's best known novel, Conrad in Quest of His Youth, Barrie states
there never was a writer so notably "the novelists'
novelist" to whom the reading public paid so little
attention. His appreciative introduction is generous,
lightened by deft touches of humor, and written in
a style calculated to win friends for the novel to
which it stands as a preface. The reading public's
interest was aroused, particularly in the United
States. In 1925, when Merrick made a second visit
to this country, he said at a dinner in his honor,
"I came simply because I love the American public
for reading my books."

INTRODUCTORY NOTE BY JAMES M. BARRIE

to Leonard Merrick's
Conrad in Search of His Youth

A disquieting sentimental journey would be doing down
the obituary column of The Times in search of the novel-
readers who have gone and died without ever knowing of the
sentimental quest of Conrad. They would be the great majority, it seems, and we may drop a sigh for them or a
"Serve you right," according to their opportunities. Incom-
plete lives.

It is from such reflections by a number of Mr. Merrick's fellow-writers that this edition of his books has sprung,
of which Conrad in Quest of His Youth is the first volume.
Disagreeing among themselves on most matters, probably
even on the value of each other to the State, they are agreed
on this, that Mr. Merrick is one of the flowers of their
calling; and they have, perhaps, an uneasy feeling that if
the public will not take his works to their hearts there must
be something wrong with the popularity of their own. "Unless you like Merrick also, please not to like me." Or
we may put it more benignantly in this way, that as you,
the gentle reader, have been good to us, we want to be good
to you, and so we present to you, with our compliments,
just about the best thing we have got--an edition of Mr.

15

Merrick's novels. There have been many "author's editions," but never, so far as I know, one quite like this, in
which the "author" is not the writer himself but his contemporaries, who have entirely "engineered" the edition
themselves and have fallen over each other, so to speak, in
this desire to join in the honour of writing the prefaces.
Such is the unique esteem in which Mr. Merrick is held by
his fellow-workers. For long he has been the novelists'
novelist, and we give you again the chance to share him with
us; you have been slow to take the previous chances, and
you may turn away again, but in any case he will still remain our man.

I speak, of course, only for myself, but there is no
doubt to my mind that Conrad in Quest of His Youth is the
best sentimental journey that has been written in this country since the publication of the other one; so gay it is, so
sad, of such an alluring spirit, so firm a temper, I know
no novel by any living Englishman except a score or so of
Mr. Hardy's, that I would rather have written. I am not
certain, however, that had the attractive choice been given
me I would not first have "knocked off" some of Mr. Merrick's short stories--particularly the Parisian ones of which
Mr. Locke will have something to say--to make sure of my
fortune in case a street accident, say, should end me a-
bruptly. In some of the other books the women, at least,
are more elaborately drawn, and there is a genuine contact
with life--Mr. Merrick with his coat off--but if, like the
shipwrecked lady in a horrible tale, I were given a moment
to decide which of my children I should save, I would on the
whole keep grip of Conrad and the short stories and let the
other babies go. Several other authors would, I am sure,
see to it that while they themselves floated, Cynthia did not
sink, and I can picture Mr. Howells diving recklessly after
The Actor-Manager.

Of my free will nothing would induce me to give away
the story of Conrad in Quest of His Youth to those who are
about to read it for the first time. I have just re-read it,
and it is as fresh as yesterday's shower; time, I am sure,
is not going to dim it; it does so effectually what we should
all have liked to try to do with it had we wakened some glad
morn with the idea, that no one need ever seek to do it again.
We must all henceforth try something else. And yet it has
been in existence for many years and comparatively few peo-

ple know of it. The libraries might issue it to the readers
of six a week as fresh from the press, with a fair chance
of not being found out. The same might be said of Mr. Hud-
son's The Purple Land, another of the choicest things of our
latter-day literature. Yet the public does not back away
from all good things even when the maker is alive; what
makes it so shy of these?

I have heard Mr. Merrick called a pessimist, and
readers are not prepared, as a rule, to spend joyous hours
with pessimists. But compared to many of his contemporaries he is quite a gay dog, laughter shining constantly in
his pages and a fine serenity; instead of setting forth to
make his characters miserable he is so much in sympathy
with them that I can think of no novelist who spends more
time--it is almost divertingly obvious--in seeking a happy
way out for them. It is as if he were fighting for some
comfort for himself, as no doubt he is. He is not always
successful, the stern artist in him forbidding, but never
were characters who, if they go hopelessly wrong, have
brought it more certainly on themselves. The author is
ever nudging them in the right direction, and never gives up
hope until the end. This must be one reason why his people are so curiously alive.

There is no such thing as a plot in his books.

"In tragic life, God wot,
No villain need be! Passions spin the plot,"

and, indeed, he is a writer of comedies always, tho' tragedy
lurks at all the corners. He has not found plot in life, and
so it cannot come into his books; if he introduced it he would
certainly be blown up by it. But there is no one with a
greater art of telling a story, if that art consists in making
us for ever wonder what we are to find on the next page.
There are a hundred surprises in Conrad. Even when you
have travelled with him far and know precisely in what circumstances he is next to be placed, shut the book and ask
yourself what is to happen and you will find you don't know
in the least; twenty lines from the close you have no idea
how the story is to end. This is the aim--perhaps the sole
aim--of the sensational writer, but he is satisfied if he has
tricked us, and we lay his tale aside, smiling at the clever
trick which is no trick as soon as he shows his hand. In

the story of character such as Conrad, there is an absence of all cheap guile; the end is merely foreseen by the author, and not by us, because he knows his people better than we do.   When we come to the end we must feel that there was no other, that he has merely discovered the truth.   Nothing is quite so fascinating, in novel-reading, as trying, as it were, to make up on an author who keeps one step in front in this way; and it doubtless accounts for the lady who accepted the hand of a publisher on condition that he told her, as a wedding gift, how a certain tale, then running in his magazine, was to end.   Very likely this is how all publishers get married.

There is, however, one way in which Mr. Merrick is such a failure that the very meanest of us can point the finger of scorn at him.   If he has a mission it is to warn us against authorship and the tawdry glamour of the stage. Could he gather all young men and maids around him he would tell them not to be authors, and if they must be authors, not to seek their characters among those who follow that bitter profession; as for the stage, he knows the seamy side of it as it never has been known to any other novelist, and he casts the light of pitiless day on it and stabs it and "wriggles his knife in the wound"; there can be no glamour in the stage for you after you have read the books of Mr. Merrick.   Obviously he hopes so, and you are a dullard indeed, if, after a dose of him, you do not see that the game is up, that you should burn your pen and avoid the stage-door for ever more.   But after you have all fled the two damned callings, I see one figure stealing back to them, raging at them, but faithful to them to the end, loving the one as his life's work and wrapt hopelessly in the glamour of the other.   Mr. Merrick is fighting his temperament in all his books and it always wins.

J. M. BARRIE.

EDMUND BLUNDEN

There is no doubt that John Clare (1793-1864),
sometimes called the English Burns, was an extraordinarily talented man, but a tragic one at that.
His strength lay in his remarkable facility for writing verse with great imagination and delight about the
natural life which surrounded him in his native parish of Helpston, England. Richard LeGalliene observed that "he embodied the accuracy of a keen-
eyed naturalist with a charming home quality of a
country lad's instinctive observation and half-con-
scious love of familiar country things, the knowledge that comes of bird-nesting and setting traps
and tickling for trout." Robert Graves spoke of him
as "a nine days' wonder who had clay on his boots,
hayseed in his hair, genius in his eye, spoke as
charmingly odd a dialect as Burns, yet had the ability to forge a neat, melodious pastoral rhyme." One
might add that he was handsome and well read in
contemporary writings of his day, both of which may
have predisposed the reading public to favor him.
John Clare's poetry burst upon the English literary scene with the publication in 1820 of Poems
Descriptive of Rural Life and Scenery, when he had
the dubious fortune to attract John Taylor, the publisher of Keats and Lamb, as his publisher. Three
editions of his Poems appeared between January 16
and the end of March, 1820. The reviewers ac-
claimed him widely although not all were enthusiastic; some were patronizing. Unfortunately this sudden burst of popularity did not last. For the next
hundred years Clare's poetry largely passed into oblivion. Fashion and a fickle public had much to do
with it. Robert Lynd expressed it laconically, "The

public blew a bubble, and the bubble burst." Thoroughly depressed by his short-lived popularity, his inability to support a growing family, and abandonment by his newly acquired literary companionship, Clare suffered a mental breakdown and was committed to an asylum where he remained for the rest of his life. Ironically, perhaps, it was here that he wrote some of his best and most melodious poems, and it may be that his asylum days, where he was treated with kindness and understanding, brought a measure of peace.

Several modern editions and selections of Clare's poetry have been published and the critical writings now extend to a full library shelf. Although not the first of the modern editions, Edmund Blunden and Alan Porter's edition of John Clare: Poems, Chiefly from Manuscript, published in 1920 by Cobden-Sanderson of London, was the first of major importance to prompt a new appraisal of Clare's work. Edmund Gosse spoke of Blunden as the discoverer of Clare, but added that Blunden's helping hand did not betray him "into a riot of hyperbole." Biographical works and critical editions of Clare's poetry and other writings within recent years all pay tribute to Blunden's "passionate commitment" to raising the esteem of Clare among British poets and restoring the honor which fate withheld during his lifetime.

In John Clare: Poems Chiefly from Manuscript, which interestingly enough appeared exactly one hundred years after the publication of Clare's first published book of poems, Blunden and Porter printed a large number of hitherto unpublished poems and revealed the existence of additional manuscripts stored at Peterborough and Northampton. Blunden provided a sensitive and sympathetic introduction to the edition which included newly discovered facts about the poet's life. Four years later he edited another selection of poems under the title Madrigals and Chronicles and in 1930, Sketches in the Life of John Clare. If one were asked to select John Clare's best work, he would most likely find himself selecting from the same poems that Blunden included in the two collections mentioned above. In a foreword to Madrigals and Chronicles Blunden

spoke of the principal characteristic of Clare's poetry as an "unparalleled intimacy" with the nature of
the English landscape.   Clare lived in a kind of
dream world.   Anyone who goes for poetry and nothing else, with nature as his pleasure, will find it in
John Clare.

from BIOGRAPHICAL INTRODUCTION
BY EDMUND BLUNDEN

to John Clare: Poems Chiefly from Manuscript

... John Clare was born on the 13th of July, 1793, in
a small cottage degraded in popular tradition to a mud hut of
the parish of Helpston, between Peterborough and Stamford.
This cottage is standing to-day, almost as it was when Clare
lived there; so that those who care to do so may examine
Martin's description of "a narrow wretched hut, more like a
prison than a human dwelling," in face of the facts.   Clare's
father, a labourer named Parker Clare, was a man with his
wits about him, whether educated or not; and Ann his wife is
recorded to have been a woman of much natural ability and
precise habits, who thought the world of her son John.   Of
the other children, little is known but that there were two
who died young and one girl who was alive in 1824.   Clare
himself wrote a sonnet in the London Magazine for June,
1821, "To a Twin Sister, Who Died in Infancy."

Parker Clare, a man with some reputation as a
wrestler and chosen for thrashing corn on account of his
strength, sometimes shared the fate of almost all farm la-
bourers of his day and was compelled to accept parish relief:
at no time can he have been many shillings to the good: but
it was his determination to have John educated to the best of
his power.   John Clare therefore attended a dame-school until he was seven; thence, he is believed to have gone to a
day-school, where he made progress enough to receive on
leaving the warm praise of the schoolmaster, and the advice
to continue at a night-school--which he did.   His aim, he
notes later on, was to write copperplate: but there are evi-
dences that he learned much more than penmanship.   Out of
school he appears to have been a happy, imaginative child:
as alert for mild mischief as the rest of the village boys, but

21

with something solitary and romantic in his disposition. One
day indeed at a very early age he went off to find the horizon;
and a little later while he tended sheep and cows in his holi-
day-time on Helpston Common, he made friends with a curious old lady called Granny Bains, who taught him old songs
and ballads. Such poems as "Childhood" and "Remembrances"
prove that Clare's early life was not mere drudgery and despair. "I never had much relish for the pastimes of youth.
Instead of going out on the green at the town end on winter
Sundays to play football I stuck to my corner stool poring
over a book; in fact, I grew so fond of being alone at last
that my mother was fain to force me into company, for the
neighbours had assured her mind ... that I was no better
than crazy.... I used to be very fond of fishing, and of a
Sunday morning I have been out before the sun delving for
worms in some old weed-blanketed dunghill and steering off
across the wet grain ... till I came to the flood-washed
meadow stream.... And then the year used to be crowned
with its holidays as thick as the boughs on a harvest home. "
It is probable that the heavy work which he is said to have
done as a child was during the long holiday at harvest-time.
When he was twelve or thirteen he certainly became team-
leader, and in this employment he saw a farm labourer fall
from the top of his loaded wagon and break his neck. For
a time his reason seemed affected by the sight.

    ... Read, mark, learn as Clare might, no opportunity
came for him to enter a profession. "After I had done with
going to school it was proposed that I should be bound apprentice to a shoemaker, but I rather disliked this bondage.
I whimpered and turned a sullen eye on every persuasion,
till they gave me my will. A neighbour then offered to learn
me his trade--to be a stone mason,--but I disliked this
too.... I was then sent for to drive the plough at Wood-
croft Castle of Oliver Cromwell memory; though Mrs. Bel-
lairs the mistress was a kind-hearted woman, and though the
place was a very good one for living, my mind was set
against it from the first; ... one of the disagreeable things
was getting up so early in the morning, ... and another was
getting wetshod ... every morning and night--for in wet
weather the moat used to overflow the causeway that led to
the porch, and as there was but one way to the house we
were obliged to wade up to the knees to get in and out....
I staid here one month, and then on coming home to my
parents they could not persuade me to return. They now

gave up all hopes of doing any good with me and fancied that
I should make nothing but a soldier; but luckily in this dilemma a next-door neighbour at the Blue Bell, Francis
Gregory, wanted me to drive plough, and as I suited him,
he made proposals to hire me for a year--which as it had
my consent my parents readily agreed to. " There he spent
a year in light work with plenty of leisure for his books and
his long reveries in lonely favourite places. His imagination
grew intensely, and in his weekly errand to a flour-mill at
Maxey ghosts rose out of a swamp and harried him till he
dropped. This stage was hardly ended when one day on his
road he saw a young girl named Mary Joyce, with whom he
instantly fell in love. This crisis occurred when Clare was
almost sixteen: the fate of John Clare hung in the balance
for six months. Then Mary's father, disturbed principally
by the chance that his daughter might be seen talking to this
erratic youngster, put an end to their meetings. From this
time, with intervals of tranquility, Clare was to suffer the
slow torture of remorse, until at length deliberately yielding
himself up to his amazing imagination he held conversation
with Mary, John Clare's Mary, his first wife Mary--as
though she had not lived unwed, and had not been in her
grave for years.

But this was not yet; and we must return to the boy
Clare, now terminating his year's hiring at the Blue Bell.
It was time for him to take up some trade in good earnest;
accordingly, in an evil hour disguised as a fortunate one, he
was apprenticed to the head gardener at Burghley Park. The
head gardener was in practice a sot and a slave-driver.
After much drunken wild bravado, not remarkable in the lad
Clare considering his companions and traditions, there came
the impulse to escape; with the result that Clare and a companion were shortly afterwards working in a nursery garden
at Newark-upon-Trent. Both the nursery garden and "the
silver Trent" are met again in the poems composed in his
asylum days; but for the time being they meant little to him,
and he suddenly departed through the snow. Arrived home
at Helpston, he lost no time in finding farm work and in writing verses: sharing a loft at night with a fellow-labourer,
he would rise at all hours to note down new ideas.

... In 1813 he read among other things the "Eikon
Basilike, " and turned his hand to odd jobs as they presented
themselves. His life appears to have been comfortable and

a little dull for a year or two; flirtation, verse-making, ambitions and his violin took their turns amiably enough! At
length he went to work in a lime-kiln several miles from
Helpston, and wrote only less poems than he read: one day
in the autumn of 1817, he was dreaming yet new verses
when he first saw "Patty," his wife-to-be. She was then
eighteen years old, and modestly beautiful; for a moment
Clare forgot Mary Joyce, and though "the courtship ultimately took a more prosaic turn," there is no denying the
fact that he was in love with "Patty" Turner, the daughter of
the small farmer who held Walkherd Lodge. In the case of
Clare, poetry was more than ever as time went on autobiography; and it is noteworthy that among the many love lyrics
addressed to Mary Joyce there are not wanting affectionate
tributes to his faithful wife Patty.

> Maid of Walkherd, meet again,
> By the wilding in the glen....
>
> And I would go to Patty's cot
>   And Patty came to me;
> Each knew the other's very thought
>   Under the hawthorn tree....
> And I'll be true for Patty's sake
>   And she'll be true for mine;
> And I this little ballad make,
>   To be her valentine.

Not long after seeing Patty, Clare was informed by
the owner of the lime-kiln that his wages would now be seven
shillings a week, instead of nine. He therefore left this
master and found similar work in the village of Pickworth,
where being presented with a shoemaker's bill for £3, he
entered into negotiations with a Market Deeping bookseller
regarding "Proposals for publishing by subscription a Collection of Original Trifles on Miscellaneous Subjects, Religious
and Moral, in verse, by John Clare, of Helpstone." Three
hundred proposals were printed, with a specimen sonnet well
chosen to intrigue the religious and moral; and yet the tale
of intending subscribers stood adamantly at seven. On the
face of it, then, Clare had lost one pound; had worn himself
out with distributing his prospectuses; and further had been
discharged from the lime-kiln for doing so in working hours.
His ambitions, indeed, set all employers and acquaintances
against him; and he found himself at the age of twenty-five
compelled to ask for parish relief. In this extremity, even

the idea of enlisting once more crossed his brain; then, that
of travelling to Yorkshire for employment: and at last, the
prospectus which had done him so much damage turned bene-
factor. With a few friends Clare was drinking success to
his goose-chase when there appeared two "real gentlemen"
from Stamford. One of these, a bookseller named Drury,
had chanced on the prospectus, and wished to see more of
Clare's poetry. Soon afterwards, he promised to publish a
selection, with corrections; and communicated with his relative, John Taylor, who with his partner Hessey managed the
well-known publishing business in Fleet Street. While this
new prospect was opening upon Clare, he succeeded in ob-
taining work once more, near the home of Patty; their love-
making proceeded, despite the usual thunderstorms, and the
dangerous rivalry of a certain dark lady named Betty Sell.

The bookseller Drury, though his appearance was in
such critical days timely for Clare, was not a paragon of
virtue. Without Clare's knowing it, he acquired the legal
copyright of the poems, probably by the expedient of dis-
pensing money at convenient times--a specious philanthropy,
as will be shown. At the same time he allowed Clare to
open a book account, which proved at length to be no special
advantage. And further, with striking astuteness, he found
constant difficulty in returning originals. In a note written
some ten years later, Clare regrets that "Ned Drury has got
my early vol. of MSS. I lent it him at first, but like all
my other MSS. elsewhere I could never get it again.... He
has copies of all my MSS. except those written for the
'Shepherd's Calendar.'" Nevertheless, through Drury,
Clare was enabled to meet his publisher Taylor and his in-
fluential friend of the Quarterly, Octavius Gilchrist, before
the end of 1819.

By 1818, there is no doubt, Clare had read very
deeply, and even had some idea of the classical authors
through translations. It is certain that he knew the great
English writers, probable that he possessed their works.
What appears to be a list of books which he was anxious to
sell in his hardest times includes some curious titles, with
some familiar ones. There are Cobb's Poems, Fawke's
Poems, Broom's, Mrs. Hoole's, and so on; there are also
Cowley's Works--Folio, Warton's "Milton," Waller, and a
Life of Chatterton; nor can he have been devoid of miscel-
laneous learning after the perusal of Watson's "Electricity,"

PRAISE FROM FAMOUS MEN

Aristotle's Works, Gasse's "Voyages," "Nature Display'd,"
and the European Magazine ("fine heads and plates"). His
handwriting at this time was bold and hasty; his opinions, to
judge from his uncompromising notes to Drury respecting the
text of the poems, almost cynical and decidedly his own.
Tact was essential if you would patronize Clare: you might
broaden his opinions, but you dared not assail them. Thus
the friendly Gilchrist, a high churchman, hardly set eyes on
Clare before condemning Clare's esteem for a dissenting
minister, a Mr. Holland, who understood the poet and the
poetry: it was some time before Gilchrist set eyes on Clare
again.

The year 1820 found Clare unemployed once more, but
the said Mr. Holland arrived before long with great news.
"In the beginning of January," Clare briefly puts it, "my
poems were published after a long anxiety of nearly two
years and all the Reviews, except Phillips' waste paper magazine, spoke in my favour." Most assuredly they did. The
literary world, gaping for drouth, had seen an announcement,
then an account of "John Clare, an agricultural labourer and
poet," during the previous autumn; the little cloud, no bigger
than a man's hand, in a little while seemed to usurp the
whole sky--or in other terms, three editions of "Poems Descriptive of Rural Life and Scenery" were sold between January 16 and the last of March. While this fever was raging
among the London coteries, critical fashionable, intellectual,
even the country folk round Helpston came to the conclusion
that Clare was something of a phenomenon. "In the course
of the publication," says Clare, "I had ventured to write to
Lord Milton to request leave that the volume might be dedicated to him; but his Lordship was starting into Italy and
forgot to answer it. So it was dedicated to nobody, which
perhaps might be as well. As soon as it was out, my mother
took one to Milton; when his Lordship sent a note to tell me
to bring ten more copies. On the following Sunday I went,
and after sitting awhile in the servants' hall (where I could
eat or drink nothing for thought), his Lordship sent for me,
and instantly explained the reasons why he did not answer my
letter, in a quiet unaffected manner which set me at rest.
He told me he had heard of my poems by Parson Mossop (of
Helpston), who I have since heard took hold of every opportunity to speak against my success or poetical abilities before
the book was published, and then, when it came out and others praised it, instantly turned round to my side. Lady

Milton also asked me several questions, and wished me to name any book that was a favourite; expressing at the same time a desire to give me one. But I was confounded and could think of nothing. So I lost the present. In fact, I did not like to pick out a book for fear of seeming over-reaching on her kindness, or else Shakespeare was at my tongue's end. Lord Fitzwilliam, and Lady Fitzwilliam too, talked to me and noticed me kindly, and his Lordship gave me some advice which I had done well perhaps to have noticed better than I have. He bade me beware of booksellers and warned me not to be fed with promises. On my departure they gave me a handful of money--the most that I had ever possessed in my life together. I almost felt I should be poor no more--there was £17. " Such is Clare's description of an incident which has been rendered in terms of insult. Other invitations followed, the chief practical result being an annuity of fifteen pounds promised by the Marquis of Exeter. Men of rank and talent wrote letters to Clare, or sent him books: some found their way to Helpston, and others sent tracts to show him the way to heaven. And now at last Clare was well enough off to marry Patty, before the birth of their first child, Anna Maria.

Before his marriage, probably, Clare was desired to spend a few days with his publisher Taylor in London. In smock and gaiters he felt most uncertain of himself and borrowed a large overcoat from Taylor to disguise his dress: over and above this question of externals, he instinctively revolted against being exhibited. Meeting Lord Radstock, sometime admiral in the Royal Navy, at dinner in Taylor's house, Clare gained a generous if somewhat religiose friend, with the instant result that he found himself "trotting from one drawing-room to the other. " He endured this with patience, thinking possibly of the cat killed by kindness; and incidentally Radstock introduced him to the strangely superficial-genuine lady Mrs. Emmerson, who was to be a faithful, thoughtful friend to his family for many years to come. In another direction, soon after Clare's return to Helpston, the retired admiral did him a great service, opening a private subscription list for his benefit: it was found possible to purchase "£250 Navy 5 Per Cents" on the 28th April and a further "£125 Navy 5 Per Cents" a month or so later. This stock, held by trustees, yielded Clare a dividend of £18 15s. at first, but in 1823 this income dwindled to £15 15s. ; and by 1832 appears to have fallen to £13 10s. To the varying amount thus derived, and to the £15 given yearly by the Marquis of Exeter, a Stamford doctor named Bell--one of Clare's most energetic admirers--succeeded in adding another annuity of £10 settled upon the poet by Lord Spencer. But in the consideration of these bounties, it is just to examine the actual financial effect of Clare's first book. The publishers' own account, furnished only through Clare's repeated demands in 1829 or thereabouts, has a sobering tale to tell: but so far no biographer has condescended to examine it.

On the first edition Clare got nothing. Against him is entered the item "Cash paid Mr. Clare for copyright p. Mr. Drury ... £20"; but this money if actually paid had been paid in 1819. Against him also is charged a curious "Commission 5 p. Cent ... £8 12s.," while Drury and Taylor acknowledge sharing profits of £26 odd.

On the second and third editions Clare got nothing; but to his account is charged the £100 which Taylor and Hessey "subscribed" to his fund. "Commission," "Advertising," "Sundries," and "Deductions allowed to Agents," account for a further £51 of the receipts: and Drury and Taylor ostensibly take over £30 apiece.

The fourth edition not being exhausted, the account is not closed: but "Advertising" has already swollen to £30, and there is no sign that Clare benefits a penny piece. Small wonder that at the foot of these figures he has written, "How can this be? I never sold the poems for any price--what money I had of Drury was given me on account of profits to be received--but here it seems I have got nothing and am brought in minus twenty pounds of which I never received a sixpence--or it seems that by the sale of these four thousand copies I have lost that much--and Drury told me that 5,000 copies had been printed tho' 4,000 only are accounted for." Had Clare noticed further an arithmetical discrepancy which apparently shortened his credit balance by some £27, he might have been still more sceptical.

Not being overweighted, therefore, with instant wealth, Clare returned to Helpston determined to continue his work in the fields. But fame opposed him: all sorts and conditions of Lydia Whites, Leo Hunters, Stigginses, and Jingles crowded to the cottage, demanding to see the Northamptonshire Peasant, and often wasting hours of his time. One day, for example, "the inmates of a whole boarding-school, located at Stamford, visited the unhappy poet"; and even more congenial visitors who cheerfully hurried him off to the tavern parlour were the ruin of his work. Yet he persevered, writing his poems only in his leisure, until the harvest of 1820 was done; then in order to keep his word with Taylor, who had agreed to produce a new volume in the spring of 1821, he spent six months in the most energetic literary labour. Writing several poems a day as he roamed the field or sat in Lea Close Oak, he would sit till late in the night sifting, recasting and transcribing. His library, by his own enterprise and by presents from many friends, was greatly enlarged, and he already knew not only the literature of the past, but also that of the present. In his letters to Taylor are mentioned his appreciations of Keats, "Poor Keats, you know how I reverence him," Shelley, Hunt, Lamb--and almost every other contemporary classic. Nor was he afraid to criticize Scott with freedom in a letter to Scott's friend Sherwell: remarking also that Wordsworth's Sonnet on Westminster Bridge had no equal in the language, but disagreeing with "his affected godliness."

Taylor and Hessey for their part did not seem over-anxious to produce the new volume of poems, perhaps because Clare would not allow any change except in the jots and tittles of his work, perhaps thinking that the public had had a surfeit of sensation. At length in the autumn of 1821 the "Village Minstrel" made its appearance, in two volumes costing twelve shillings; with the bait of steel engravings, -- the first, an unusually fine likeness of Clare from the painting by Hilton; the second, an imaginative study of Clare's cottage, not without representation of the Blue Bell, the village cross and the church. The book was reviewed less noisily, and a sale of a mere 800 copies in two months was regarded as "a very modified success." Meanwhile, Clare was writing for the London Magazine, and Cherry tells us that "as he contributed almost regularly for some time, a substantial addition was made to his income." Clare tells us, in a note on a cash account dated 1827, "In this cash account there is nothing allowed me for my three years' writing for the London Magazine. I was to have £12 a year."

... In May, 1822, Clare spent a brief holiday in London, meeting there the strong men of the London Magazine,

Lamb, Hood, and the rest. From his clothes, the <u>London</u>
group called him The Green Man; Lamb took a singular interest in him, and was wont to address him as "Clarissimus"
and "Princely Clare." Another most enthusiastic acquaintance
was a painter named Rippingille, who had begun life as the
son of a farmer at King's Lynn, and who was not thoroughly
capable of taking Clare into the most Bohemian corners of
London. Suddenly, however, news came from Helpston recalling the poet from these perambulations, and he returned
in haste, to find his second daughter born, Eliza Louisa,
god-child of Mrs. Emmerson and Lord Radstock.

At this time, Clare appears to have been writing ballads of a truly rustic sort, perhaps in the light of his universal title, The Northamptonshire Peasant Poet. He would
now, moreover, collect such old ballads and songs as his
father and mother or those who worked with him might chance
to sing; but was often disappointed to find that "those who
knew fragments seemed ashamed to acknowledge it ... and
those who were proud of their knowledge in such things knew
nothing but the senseless balderdash that is brawled over and
sung at country feasts, statutes, and fairs, where the most
senseless jargon passes for the greatest excellence, and ru-
dest indecency for the finest wit." None the less he recovered sufficient material to train himself into the manner
of these "old and beautiful recollections." But whatever he
might write or edit, he was unlikely to find publishers willing
to bring out. The "Village Minstrel" had barely passed the
first thousand, and the "second edition" was not melting away.
Literature after all was not money, and to increase Clare's
anxiety and dilemma came illness. In the early months of
1823, he made a journey to Stamford to ask the help of his
old friend Gilchrist. Gilchrist was already in the throes of
his last sickness, and Clare took his leave without a word of
his own difficulties. Arriving home, he fell into a worse illness than before; but as the spring came on he rallied, and
occasionally walked to Stamford to call on his friend, who
likewise seemed beginning to mend. On the 30th of June,
Clare was received with the news "Mr. Gilchrist is dead."
Clare relapsed into a curious condition which appeared likely
to overthrow his life or his reason when Taylor most fortunately came to see him, and procured him the best doctor
in Peterborough. This doctor not only baffled Clare's disease, but, rousing attention wherever he could in the neighbourhood, was able to provide him with good food and even

some old port from the cellar of the Bishop of Peterborough.

At last on the advice of the good doctor and the renewed invitation of Taylor, Clare made a third pilgrimage to
London, and this time stayed from the beginning of May till
the middle of July, 1824.   Passing the first three weeks in
peaceful contemplation of London crowds, he was well enough
then to attend a London Magazine dinner, where De Quincey
swam into his ken, and the next week a similar gathering
where Coleridge talked for three hours.   Clare sat next to
Charles Elton and gained a staunch friend, who shortly
afterwards sent him a letter in verse with a request that he
should sit to Rippingille for his portrait:

> His touch will, hue by hue, combine
> Thy thoughtful eyes, that steady shine,
> The temples of Shakesperian line,
> The quiet smile.

To J. H. Reynolds he seemed "a very quiet and worthy yet
enthusiastic man. "   George Darley, too, was impressed by
Clare the man, and for some time was to be one of the few
serious critics of Clare the poet.   Allan Cunningham showed
a like sympathy and a still more active interest.   A less
familiar character, the journalist Henry Van Dyk, perhaps
did Clare more practical good than either.

With these good effects of Clare's third visit to town,
another may be noted.   A certain Dr. Darling attended him
throughout, and persuaded him to give up drink; this he did.
The real trouble at Helpston was to discover employment,
for already Clare was supporting his wife, his father and
mother, and three young children.   Farmers were unwilling
to employ Clare, indeed insulted him if he applied to them:
and his reticence perhaps lost him situations in the gardens
of the Marquis of Exeter, and then of the Earl Fitzwilliam.
In spite of disappointments, he wrote almost without pause,
sometimes making poems in the manner of elder poets (with
the intention of mild literary forgery), sometimes writing in
his normal vein for the lately announced "New Shepherd's
Calendar"; and almost daily preparing two series of articles,
on natural history and on British birds.   A curious proof of
the facility with which he wrote verse is afforded by the great
number of rhymed descriptions of birds, their nests and eggs
which this period produced: as though he sat down resolved

to write prose notes and found his facts running into metre
even against his will. As if not yet embroiled in schemes
enough, Clare planned and began a burlesque novel, an autobiography, and other prose papers: while he kept a diary
which should have been published. Clare had been forced
into a literary career, and no one ever worked more consci-
entiously or more bravely. Those who had at first urged
him to write can scarcely be acquitted of desertion now:
but the more and the better Clare wrote, the less grew the
actual prospect of production, success and independence.

... In June, 1826, his fourth child was born, and
Clare entreated Taylor to bring out the "Shepherd's Calendar, " feeling that he might at least receive money enough for
the comfort of his wife and his baby; but Taylor felt otherwise, recommending Clare to write for the annuals which now
began to flourish. This Clare at last persuaded himself to
do. Payment was tardy, and in some cases imaginary; and
for the time being the annuals were not the solution of his
perplexities. He therefore went back to the land; and bor-
rowing the small means required rented at length a few
acres, with but poor results.

The publication of Clare's first book had been managed
with excellent strategy; Taylor had left nothing to chance,
and the public responded as he had planned. The independence of Clare may have displeased the publisher; at any rate,
his enthusiasm dwindled, and further to jeopardize Clare's
chances it occurred that in 1825 Taylor and Hessey came to
an end, the partners separating. Omens were indeed bad
for the "Shepherd's Calendar" which, two years after its announcement, in June, 1827, made its unobtrusive appearance.
There were very few reviews, and the book sold hardly at
all. Yet this was conspicuously finer work than Clare had
done before. Even "that beautiful frontispiece of De Wint's, "
as Taylor wrote, did not attract attention. The forgotten
poet, slaving at his small-holding, found that his dream had
come true. Meanwhile Allan Cunningham had been inquiring
into this non-success, and early in 1828 wrote to Clare
urging him to come to London and interview the publisher.
An invitation from Mrs. Emmerson made the visit possible.
Once more then did Clare present himself at 20, Stratford
Place, and find his "sky chamber" ready to receive him.
Nor did he allow long time to elapse before finding out Allan
Cunningham, who heartily approved of his plan to call on

Taylor, telling him to request a full statement of account.
The next day, when Clare was on the point of making the
demand, Taylor led across the trail with an unexpected offer; recommending Clare to buy the remaining copies of his
"Shepherd's Calendar" from him at half-a-crown each, that
he might sell them in his own district. Clare asked time
to reflect. A week later, against the wish of Allan Cunningham, he accepted the scheme.

Clare had had another object in coming to town. Dr.
Darling had done him so much good on a previous occasion
that he wished to consult him anew. On the 25th of February, 1828, Clare wrote to his wife: "Mr. Emmerson's doctor, a Mr. Ward, told me last night there was little or
nothing the matter with me--and yet I got no sleep the whole
of last night. " Already, it appears, had coldness and dilemma unsettled him. That they had not subdued him, and that
his home life was in the main happy and affectionate, and of
as great an importance to him as any of his aspirations, is
to be judged from his poems and his letters of 1828 and
thereabouts.

... But now Clare is home at Helpston, ready with a
sack of poetry to tramp from house to house and try his luck.
Sometimes he dragged himself thirty miles a day, meeting
rectors who "held it unbecoming to see poems hawked about":
one day, having walked seven miles into Peterborough, and
having sold no books anywhere, he trudged home to find Patty
in the pains of labour; and now had to go back to Peterborough
as fast as he might for a doctor. Now there were nine living beings dependent on Clare. At length he altered his plan
of campaign, and advertised that his poems could be had at
his cottage, with some success. About this time Clare was
invited to write for "The Spirit of the Age, " and still he supplied brief pieces to the hated but unavoidable annuals.
Letters too from several towns in East Anglia, summoning
John Clare with his bag of books, at least promised him
some slight revenue; actually he only went to one of these
places, namely Boston, where the mayor gave a banquet in
his honour, and enabled him to sell several volumes--auto-
graphed. Among the younger men, a similar feast was proposed; but Clare declined, afterwards reproaching himself
bitterly on discovering that they had hidden ten pounds in his
wallet. On his return home not only himself but the rest of
the family in turn fell ill with fever, so that the spring of

1829 found Clare out of work and faced with heavy doctor's-bills.

Intellectually, John Clare was in 1828 and 1829 probably at his zenith. He had ceased long since to play the poetic ploughman; he had gained in his verses something more ardent and stirring than he had shown in the "Shepherd's Calendar"; and the long fight (for it was nothing less) against leading-strings and obstruction now began to manifest itself in poems of regret and of soliloquy. Having long written for others' pleasure, he now wrote for his own nature.

> I would not wish the burning blaze
> Of fame around a restless world,
> The thunder and the storm of praise
> In crowded tumults heard and hurled.

There had been few periods of mental repose since 1820. His brain and his poetic genius, by this long discipline and fashioning, were now triumphant together. The declension from this high estate might have been more abrupt but for the change in his fortunes. He had again with gentleness demanded his accounts from his publisher, and when in August, 1829, these accounts actually arrived, disputed several points and gained certain concessions: payment was made from the editors of annuals; and with these reliefs came the chance for him to rent a small farm and to work on the land of Earl Fitzwilliam. His working hours were long, and his mind was forced to be idle. This salutary state of affairs lasted through 1830, until happiness seemed the only possibility before him. What poems he wrote occurred suddenly and simply to him. His children--now six in number--were growing up in more comfort and in more prospect than he had ever enjoyed. But he reckoned not with illness.

In short, illness reduced Clare almost to skin-and-bone. Farming not only added nothing but made encroachment on his small stipend. In despair he flung himself into field labour again, and was carried home nearly dead with fever. Friends there were not wanting to send food and medicine; Parson Mossop, having long ago been converted to Clare, did much for him. Even so the landlord distrained for rent, and Clare applied to his old friend Henderson the botanist at Milton Park. Lord Milton came by and Clare was encouraged to tell him his trouble; his intense phrases and bearing were such that the nobleman at once promised him a new cottage and a plot of ground. At the same time, he expressed his hope that there would soon be another volume of poems by John Clare. This hope was the spark which fired a dangerous train, perhaps; for Clare once again fell into his exhausting habit of poetry all the day and every day. He decided to publish a new volume by subscription.

... In his new home Clare was for a time troubled with visitors; to most he was aloof, but sometimes he spoke freely of his affairs.... With the gear that Mrs. Emmerson's kindness and activity had provided, Clare kept his garden and ground in order; yet the winter of 1832 was a time of great hardship and foreboding. His youngest son Charles was born on the 4th of January, 1833; the event shook Clare's nerve more terribly perhaps than anything before had done and he went out into the fields. Late in the day his daughter Anna found him lying unconscious, and for a month he had to keep his bed. As if to prove the proverb "It never rains but it pours, " subscribers to his new volume hung back, and when spring had come they numbered in all forty-nine. Clare submitted the work to the publishers, great and small, but the best offer that he got depended on his providing in advance £100 for the necessary steel engravings. And now Clare lost all his delight in lonely walks, but sitting in his study wrote curious paraphrases of "the Psalms, the Proverbs, and the Book of Job. " His manner towards those round him became apathetic and silent. Even the news brought by his doctor--who prescribed Clare to his other patients--that subscribers now were more than two hundred, seemed to sound meaningless in his ears. But even these danger-signs seemed discounted by the self-command and cheerfulness which Clare soon afterwards regained; and ashamed of his misjudgment, Dr. Smith came to the conclusion that he need visit Clare no more. An attack of insanity immediately followed, during which Clare did not know his wife, his children or himself.

From this heavy trance he awoke, bitterly aware of his peril. He wrote at once to Taylor, again and again. "You must excuse my writing; but I feel that if I do not write now I shall not be able. What I wish is to get under Dr. Darling's advice, or to have his advice to go somewhere; for I have not been from home this twelvemonth, and cannot get anywhere. " ... "If I could but go to London, I think I should get better. How would you advise me to come? I

35

dare not come up by myself.   Do you think one of my children might go with me?   ...   Thank God my wife and children are all well. "   Taylor wrote once in mildly sympathetic
words, but probably thought that Clare was making much ado
about nothing.   And here at least was the opportunity for a
patron to save a poet from death-in-life for five pounds.
Nothing was done, and Clare sat in his study, writing more
and more paraphrases of the Old Testament, together with
series of sonnets of a grotesque, rustic sort, not resembling
any other poems in our language.

The "Midsummer Cushion" had been set aside, but
Clare had submitted many of the poems together with hundreds more to Messrs. Whittaker.   Largely through the
recommendations of Mr. Emmerson, the publishers decided
to print a volume from these, picking principally those poems
which had already shown themselves respectable by appearing
in the annuals.   One even written in 1820, "The Autumn
Robin, " was somehow chosen, to the exclusion of such later
poems as "Remembrances" and "The Fallen Elm. "   With
faults like these, the selection was nevertheless a distinctly
beautiful book of verse.   In March, 1834, Clare definitely
received forty pounds for the copyright, and finally in July,
1835, appeared this his last book, "The Rural Muse. "   Its
success was half-hearted, in spite of a magnificent eulogy by
Christopher North in Blackwood's, and of downright welcome
by the Athenoeum, the New Monthly and other good judges.
There was a slow sale for several months, but for Clare
there was little chance of new remuneration.   This he could
regard calmly, for while the book was in the press he had
received from the Literary Fund a present of fifty pounds.

Clare's malady slowly increased.   The exact history
of this decline is almost lost, yet we may well believe that
the death of his mother on the 18th of December, 1835, was
a day of double blackness for him.   The winter over, Patty
made a great fight for his reason, and at last persuaded him
to go out for walks, which checked the decline.   Now he became so passionately fond of being out-of-doors that "he
could not be made to stop a single day at home. "   In one of
these roving walks he met his old friend Mrs. Marsh, the
wife of the Bishop of Peterborough.   A few nights later as
her guest he sat in the Peterborough theatre watching the
"Merchant of Venice. "   So vivid was his imagination--for
doubtless the strolling players were not in themselves con-

vincing--that he at last began to shout at Shylock and try to attack him on the stage. When Clare returned to Helpston, the change in him terrified his wife. And yet, he rallied and walked the fields, and sitting on the window-seat taught his sons to trim the two yew-trees in his garden into old-fashioned circles and cones. The positive signs of derangement which he had given so far were not after all conclusive. He had seen Mary Joyce pass by, he had spoken to her, occasionally he as a third person had watched and discussed the doings of John Clare and this lost sweetheart. He had surprised one or two people by calling mole-hills mountains. One day, too, at Parson Mossop's house he had suddenly pointed to figures moving up and down. Under these circumstances, a Market Deeping doctor named Skrimshaw certified him mad; and on similar grounds almost any one in the world might be clapped into an asylum.

Hallucinations ceased for a few months, but Mrs. Clare had difficulty in keeping outside interference at bay. Earl Fitzwilliam, in his position of landlord, proposed to send the man who called mole-hills mountains at once to the Northampton Asylum. When the summer came, unfortunately, Clare's mind seemed suddenly to give way, and preparations were being made for his admission to the county Asylum when letters came from Taylor and other old friends in London, proposing to place him in private hands. Clare was taken accordingly on the 16th of July, 1837, to Fair Mead House, Highbeach, in Epping Forest.

Dr. Allen, the mild broad-minded founder of this excellent asylum, had few doubts as to the condition of Clare's mind, and assured him an eventual recovery. As with the fifty other patients, so he dealt with Clare: keeping him away from books, and making him work in the garden and the fields. Poetry, it is said, was made impossible for him, paper being taken away from him; but it is not conceivable that Clare could live apart from this kindest of companions for many months together. Soon he was allowed to go out into the forest at his will, often taking his new acquaintance Thomas Campbell, the son of the poet, on these wood-rambles. His hallucinations do not appear to have diminished, although they changed. He was now convinced that Mary Joyce was his true wife--Patty was his "second wife." He had known William Shakespeare, and many other great ones in person. Why such men as Wordsworth, Campbell and

Byron were allowed to steal John Clare's best poems and to
publish them as their own, he could not imagine.   John Clare
was not only noble by nature but by blood also. --On such
rumoured eccentricities did the popular notion of his madness rest.   It would seem that anything he said was taken
down in evidence against him.   How dared he be figurative?

On the other hand, Miss Mitford records figurative
conversations not so easily explained; his eye-witness's account of the execution of Charles the First, "the most graphic
and minute, with an accuracy as to costume and manners far
exceeding what would probably have been at his command if
sane," and his seaman's narrative of the battle of the Nile
and the death of Nelson in exact nautical detail.   These imaginations she compares to clairvoyance.   Cyrus Redding, who
left three accounts of his visit, found him "no longer, as he
was formerly, attenuated and pale of complexion ... a little
man, of muscular frame and firmly set, his complexion fresh
and forehead high, a nose somewhat aquiline, and long full
chin."   "His manner was perfectly unembarrassed, his language correct and fluent; he appeared to possess great can-
dour and openness of mind, and much of the temperament of
genius.   There was about his manner no tincture of rusticity."
Once only during the conversation did Clare betray any aber-
ration, abruptly introducing and abandoning the topic of Prize-
fighting, as though "a note had got into a piece of music
which had no business there."

Clare told Redding that he missed his wife and his
home, the society of women, and books.   At last, having
been in the private asylum four years, he "returned home
out of Essex" on foot, leaving Epping Forest early on July
20, 1841, and dragging himself along almost without pause
until July 23.   Of this amazing journey he himself wrote an
account for "Mary Clare," which is printed in full in Martin's "Life": it is both in style and in subject an extraordinary document.   The first night, he says, "I lay down
with my head towards the north, to show myself the steering-
point in the morning."   On "the third day I satisfied my hun-
ger by eating the grass on the roadside which seemed to
taste something like bread.   I was hungry and eat heartily
till I was satisfied; in fact, the meal seemed to do me good."
And "there was little to notice, for the road very often
looked as stupid as myself."   At last between Peterborough
and Helpston "a cart met me, with a man, a woman and a

boy in it. When nearing me the woman jumped out, and caught fast hold of my hands, and wished me to get into the cart. But I refused; I thought her either drunk or mad. But when I was told it was my second wife, Patty, I got in, and was soon at Northborough. "

... Patty worked her hardest to keep Clare out of future asylums, but it seems that her wishes were overridden. Dr. Allen let it be known through the Gentleman's Magazine and other publications that Clare would in the ordinary way almost certainly recover: but the local doctors knew better. On the authority of an anonymous "patron" the doctor Skrimshaw who had previously found Clare insane now paid him another visit, and with a certain William Page, also of Market Deeping, condemned him to be shut up

"After years addicted to poetical prosings. "

Then one day keepers came, and a vain struggle, and the Northborough cottage saw John Clare no more. He was now in the asylum at Northampton, and the minds of Northamptonshire noblemen need no longer be troubled that a poet was wandering in miserable happiness under their park walls.

So far, the madness of Clare had been rather an exaltation of mind than a collapse. Forsaken mainly by his friends--even Mrs. Emmerson's letters ceased in 1837,--unrecognized by the new generation of writers and of readers, hated by his neighbours, wasted with hopeless love, he had encouraged a life of imagination and ideals. Imagination overpowered him, until his perception of realities failed him. He could see Mary Joyce or talk with her, he had a family of dream-children by her: but if this was madness, there was method in it. But now the blow fell, imprisonment for life: down went John Clare into idiocy, "the ludicrous with the terrible. " And even from this desperate abyss he rose.

Earl Fitzwilliam paid for Clare's maintenance in the Northampton Asylum, but at the ordinary rate for poor people. The asylum authorities at least seemed to have recognized Clare as a man out of the common, treating him as a "gentleman patient, " and allowing him--for the first twelve years--to go when he wished into Northampton, where he would sit under the portico of All Saints' Church in meditation. What dreams were these! "sometimes his face would brighten up as if illuminated by an inward sun, overwhelming in its glory and beauty." Sane intervals came, in which he wrote his poems; and these poems were of a serenity and richness not surpassed in his earlier work, including for instance "Graves of Infants" (May, 1844), "The Sleep of Spring" (1844), "Invitation to Eternity" (1848) and "Clock-a-Clay" (before 1854). But little news of him went farther afield than the town of Northampton, and the poems remained in manuscript. A glimpse of Clare in these years is left us by a Mr. Jesse Hall, who as an admirer of his poems called on him in May, 1848. "As it was a very fine day, he said we could go and have a walk in the grounds of the institution. We discussed many subjects and I found him very rational, there being very little evidence of derangement.... I asked permission for him to come to my hotel the next day. We spent a few hours together. I was very sorry to find a great change in him from the previous day, and I had ample evidence of his reason being dethroned, his conversation being disconnected and many of his remarks displaying imbecility: but at times he spoke rationally and to the point." To Hall as to almost every other casual visitor Clare gave several manuscript poems.

A letter to his wife, dated July 19th, 1848, gives fresh insight into his condition:

My Dear Wife,

I have not written to you a long while, but here I am in the land of Sodom where all the people's brains are turned the wrong way. I was glad to see John yesterday, and should like to have gone back with him, for I am very weary of being here. You might come and fetch me away, for I think I have been here long enough.

I write this in a green meadow by the side of the river agen Stokes Mill, and I see three of their daughters and a son now and then. The confusion and roar of mill dams and locks is sounding very pleasant while I write it, and it's a very beautiful evening; the meadows are greener than usual after the shower and the rivers are brimful. I think it is about two years since I was first sent up in this Hell and French Bastille of English liberty. Keep yourselves happy and comfortable and love one another. By and bye I shall be with you, perhaps before you expect me.

There has been a great storm here with thunder and hail that did much damage to the glass in the neighbourhood. Hailstones the size of hens' eggs fell in some places. Did your brother John come to Northborough or go to Barnack? His uncle John Riddle came the next morning but did not stay. I thought I was coming home but I got cheated. I see many of your little brothers and sisters at Northampton, weary and dirty with hard work; some of them with red hands, but all in ruddy good health: some of them are along with your sister Ruth Dakken who went from Helpston a little girl. Give my love to your Mother, Grandfather and Sisters, and believe me, my dear children, hers and yours,

Very affectionately
John Clare

Life went on with little incident for Clare in the asylum. To amuse himself he read and wrote continually; in 1850 his portrait was painted, and his death reported. In 1854 he assisted Miss Baker in her "Glossary of Northamptonshire Words and Phrases," providing her with all his asylum manuscripts and specially contributing some verses on May-day customs. At this time an edition of his poems was projected, and the idea met with much interest among those who yet remembered Clare: but it faded and was gone. The "harmless lunatic" was at length confined to the asylum grounds, and to the distresses of his mind began to be added those of the ageing body. Hope even now was not dead, and a poor versifier but good Samaritan who saw him in 1857 printed some lines in the London Journal for November 21st asking the aid of Heaven to restore Clare to his home and his poetry (for he seems to have written little at that time); a gentleman who was in a position to judge wrote also that in the spring of 1860 his mind was calmer than it had been for years, and that he was induced to write verses once more. But Clare was sixty-seven years old; it was perhaps too late to release him, and perhaps he had grown past the desire of liberty. On the 7th of March he wrote to Patty, asking after all his children and some of his friends, and sending his love to his father and mother (so long since dead); signing himself "Your loving husband till death, John Clare." On the 8th he wrote a note to Mr. Hopkins: "Why I am shut up I don't know." And on the 9th he answered his "dear Daughter Sophia's letter," saying that he was "not quite

so well to write" as he had been, and (presumably in reply
to some offer of books or comforts) "I want nothing from
Home to come here.   I shall be glad to see you when you
come. "   In the course of 1860 he was photographed, and
that the Northampton folk still took an interest in their poet
is proved by the sale of these likenesses; copies could be
seen in the shops until recent years.   But that Clare might
have been set at large seems not to have occurred to those
who in curiosity purchased his portrait.

   ... Clare became patriarchal in appearance; and his
powers failed more rapidly, until he could walk no longer.
A wheel-chair was procured for him, that he might still enjoy the garden and the open air.   On Good Friday in 1864,
he was taken out for the last time; afterwards he could not
be moved, yet he would still manage to reach his window-
seat; then came paralysis, and on the afternoon of May the
20th, 1864,

> His soul seemed with the free,
> He died so quietly.

   His last years had been spent in some degree of
happiness, and from officials and fellow-patients he had received gentleness, and sympathy, and even homage.   It has
been said, not once nor twice but many times, that in the
asylum he was never visited by his wife, nor by any of his
children except the youngest son, Charles, who came once.
That any one should condemn Patty for her absence is surely
presumptuous in the extreme: she was now keeping her
home together with the greatest difficulty, nor can it be
known what deeper motives influenced relationships between
wife and husband, even if the name of Mary Joyce meant
nothing.   That the children came to see their father whenever they could, the letters given above signify: but, if the
opportunities were not many, there were the strongest of
reasons.   Frederick died in 1843, just after Clare's incar-
ceration: Anna in the year following: Charles the youngest,
a boy of great promise, in 1852:   and Sophia in 1863.   William, and John who went to Wales, went when occasion came
and when they could afford the expense of the journey: Eliza, who survived last of Clare's children and who most of
all understood him and his poetry, was unable through illness to leave her home for many years, yet she went once
to see him.   The isolation which found its expression in "I

Am" was another matter: it was the sense of futility, of not
having fulfilled his mission, of total eclipse that spoke there.
N. P. Willis, perhaps the Howitts, and a few more worthies
came for brief hours to see Clare, rather as a phenomenon
than as a poet; but Clare, who had sat with Elia and his assembled host, who had held his own with the finest brains of
his time and had written such a cornucopia of genuine poetry
now lying useless in his cottage at Northborough, cannot but
have regarded the Northampton Asylum as "the shipwreck of
his own esteems. "

Clare was buried on May 25th, 1864, where he had
wished to be, in the churchyard at Helpston.   The letter in-
forming Mrs. Clare of his death was delivered at the wrong
address, and did not eventually reach her at Northborough
before Clare's coffin arrived at Helpston; scarcely giving her
time to attend the funeral the next day.   Indeed, had the sex-
ton at Helpston been at home, the bearers would have urged
him to arrange for the funeral at once; in his absence, they
left the coffin in an inn parlour for the night, and a scandal
was barely prevented.   A curious superstition grew up local-
ly that it was not Clare's body which was buried in that coffin: and among those who attended the last rite, not one but
found it almost impossible to connect this episode with those
days forty years before, when so many a notable man was
seen making through Helpston village for the cottage of the
eager-eyed, brilliant, unwearying young poet who was the
talk of London.   After such a long silence and oblivion, even
the mention of John Clare's name in his native village awoke
odd feelings of unreality.

The poetry of John Clare, originally simple description of the country and countrymen, or ungainly imitation of
the poetic tradition as he knew it through Allan Ramsay,
Burns, and the popular writers of the eighteenth century,
developed into a capacity for exact and complete nature-
poetry and for self-expression.   Thoroughly awake to all
the finest influences in life and in literature, he devoted
himself to poetry in every way.   Imagination, colour, melo-
dy and affection were his by nature; where he lacked was
in dramatic impulse and in passion, and sometimes his incredible facility in verse, which enabled him to complete
poem after poem without pause or verbal difficulty, was not
his best friend.   He possesses a technique of his own; his
rhymes are based on pronunciation, the Northamptonshire

pronunciation to which his ear had been trained, and thus he accurately joins "stoop" and "up," or "horse" and "cross"-- while his sonnets are free and often unique in form.   In spite of his individual manner, there is no poet who in his nature-poetry so completely subdues self and mood and deals with the topic for its own sake.   That he is by no means en- slaved to nature-poetry, the variety of the poems in this selection must show.

His Asylum Poems are distinct from most of the earlier work.   They are often the expressions of his love tragedy, yet strange to say they are not often sad or bitter: imagination conquers, and the tragedy vanishes.   They are rhythmically new, the movement having changed from that of quiet reflection to one of lyrical enthusiasm: even nature is now seen in brighter colours and sung in subtler music.   Old age bringing ever intenser recollection and childlike vision found Clare writing the light lovely songs which bear no slightest sign of the cruel years.   So near in these later poems are sorrow and joy that they awaken deeper feelings and instincts than almost any other lyrics can--emotions such as he shares with us in his "Adieu!":

> I left the little birds
> And sweet lowing of the herds,
> And couldn't find out words,
>   Do you see,
> To say to them good-bye,
> Where the yellowcups do lie;
> So heaving a deep sigh,
>   Took to sea....

In this sort of pathos, so indefinable and intimate, William Blake and only he can be said to resemble him.

B.

ELMER DAVIS

"This Is London, ten minutes before five in the morning. Tonight's raid has been widespread. London again is the main target." The familiar opening phrase with which Edward R. Murrow began his daily broadcasts from London during World War II is still fresh in the memory of thousands of people in this country who listened to him with gratitude and affection for his vividness, courage, and truthfulness. A selection of these broadcasts appeared in book form in 1941 under the title with which he repeatedly opened his broadcasts, with a commentary and introduction by Elmer Davis.

Murrow's short-wave reports, even when read rather than being heard, have the impact of dramatic immediacy. Some were made while the whine and explosion of bombs were spelling themselves in his ears. His memory of these raids was always fresh in his mind when he spoke on the air. His broadcasts on the Battle of Britain mention the important historical events (the signing of the German-Russian treaty, for example) but do not attempt to interpret their importance or to explain the reasons back of events. Rather they are "mood pieces," dealing almost exclusively with the people themselves, and chiefly with the "little people" of a great, besieged city. They provide quick-sketch profiles of men, women, soldiers, and civilians. They are full of anecdotes, and, above all, as Elmer Davis points out in his introduction, they reflect "the changing ideas and emotions, the hopes and the fears ... of Englishmen of every class." Londoners gave Murrow high marks for his reporting. They said he had courage and a clear eye for important detail.

Always incisive, he disciplined himself to a notable
simplicity and clarity. He had magnanimity and
compassion. As one Londoner pointed out "he had
equally the rare gift of sympathy and a deep sense
of communion, coupled with a restraint which permitted him to convey the deep emotions aroused by
events without dropping into mere sentiment."

No better choice than Elmer Davis could have
been made to provide a short introduction to Edward Murrow's writing. As reporters they had
common virtues: a passion for truth, the assur-
ance of their own convictions, and, while they may
have had doubts about the future, they had confidence in individual liberty and freedom. In 1943
Elmer Davis pointed out that the Supreme Court declared that the "fixed star in our constitutional con-
stellation" is that no American official "can prescribe what shall be orthodox politics, nationalism,
religion, or other matters of opinion." Murrow
talks about the courage of the British people in the
bloody battle for Britain, but he says that they did
not think of their individual acts as courage even
though they knew the risks involved. No one in
the United States showed more intellectual integrity
and courage than Elmer Davis in his war against
McCarthyism. He demonstrated that those years
were nothing less than a cold civil war to test
whether a nation conceived and dedicated like America could long endure. "I believe it will endure,
only if we stand up for it. The frightened men who
are trying to frighten us, because they have no faith
in their country, are wrong; and even wronger are
the smart men who are trying to use frightened men
for their own ends." A later generation might well
have thought he was referring to high offices in
Washington.

INTRODUCTION BY ELMER DAVIS

to Edward R. Murrow's
This Is London

Everyone who listens to the war news is familiar with

ELMER DAVIS

Ed Murrow's salutation, "This is London." That is what this book is about. From his broadcasts in the first sixteen months of the war these selections have been compiled not as a day-by-day history, but in the belief that this is London-- a record of what London thought and felt about a war that began as something remote and hardly real and gradually became the dominant reality of daily, and still more of nightly, life.

The selection has been made by F. W. Mordaunt Hall of the Columbia Broadcasting System's staff, and all those concerned with the production of the book applaud his choice. Yet it should be pointed out that Murrow himself might have made a different selection. The emphasis is perhaps not quite the same on the spot as at a distance; but Murrow had other things to think about, and this seems the best that could be done three thousand miles away. The reader might remember, too, that this is the language of speech, not of the printed page; all this material was designed to be heard, not read. But it is what Ed Murrow, and no one else, thought was what ought to be heard on any given date; as is explained in one of these broadcasts, the censorship under which he works is negative; it can tell him what to leave out but it never tries to tell him what to put in. And he talks under no instructions from the home office in New York except to find the news and report it.

We who work with Murrow are keenly aware of his excellence as a reporter of pure news; indeed some of us-- having, like most radio news men, learned our trade in another medium--are perhaps faintly scandalized that such good reporting can be done by a man who never worked on a newspaper in his life, and acquired his basic experience of Europe first as president of the National Student Federation of the United States and then in the service of the Institute of International Education. The only objection that can be offered to Murrow's technique of reporting is that when an air raid is on he has the habit of going up on the roof to see what is happening, or of driving around town in an open car to see what has been hit. That is a good way to get the news, but perhaps not the best way to make sure that you will go on getting it.

But news is no longer news by the time it could be printed in a book, which explains some omissions in this volume. If you want to know what Murrow had to say in certain critical periods--the first few days after the signing of the German-Russian treaty, the first few days of the Blitzkrieg in the west, and so on--you will not find it here; for on those days his broadcasts were a chronicle of events which now are history. In this compilation news has been included only if it had some ironic value or some direct bearing on the states of mind which Murrow was reporting.

For this is the unique value of his broadcasts--their reflection of the changing ideas and emotions, the hopes and the fears and the endeavors to look ahead, of Englishmen of nearly all classes, high and low. No one yet knows whether there will be a Europe fit to live in after this war; but if there is, it will be due chiefly to such Englishmen as those whose thoughts and feelings are recorded here--men who even in the stress of the struggle for survival find time occasionally to look ahead, to try to make up their minds what they want and what they may have some hope of getting if they win. It is, you may observe, a very different England (or Britain, if particularistic Scots insist on the distinction) from the Britain which was one of the characters in the drama of prewar international politics. That difference is the most hopeful thing about it.

ELMER DAVIS

February, 1941
New York

IRA DILWORTH

"I felt so young and empty standing there before the Indians and the two grave Missionaries! The Chief, old Hipi, was held to be a reader of faces. He perched himself on the top of the Missionaries' drug cupboard; his brown fists clutched the edge of it, his elbows taut and shoulders hunched. His crumpled shoes hung loose as if they dangled from strings and had no feet in them. The stare of his eyes searched me right through. Suddenly they were done; he lifted them above me to the window, uttered several terse sentences in Chinook, jumped off the cupboard and strode back to the village.

"I was half afraid to ask the Missionary, 'What did he say?'

"'Not much. Only that you had no fear, that you were not stuck up, and that you knew how to laugh.'"

This passage from Klee Wyck, published in 1941, shortly before her seventieth birthday and recalling vividly her first youthful meeting with the patriarch of a West Coast Indian village in British Columbia, is typical Emily Carr--her fearlessness, and her vivid, descriptive prose. No other book of hers, not even the posthumously published autobiography, Growing Pains, or her fascinating journal, Hundreds and Thousands, furnishes such full and happy expression of her gift for human understanding or for casually interweaving keenly observed incidents-- comic, tragic, poignant--with her response to the vitality of the art of the coastal Indians.

Emily Carr's life was a blend of convention and rebellion. She grew up in a society that was conservative, tired, and prudent and one that wanted

49

to do with anything new or strange. She loved her country passionately but it nourished her talents thinly. Born in Victoria, British Columbia, in 1871, to an English family, orphaned at an early age, she asserted her independence by persuading her guardian to let her attend a school of art in San Francisco. She returned, as she did from a visit to London a few years later, to settle down to painting and teaching art in the conventional mode of the day. When some years later she went to Paris and encountered the "new impressionism" she changed her whole approach to painting. When she returned this time with a "bigger freer seeing ... the Vancouver schools in which I had taught refused to employ me again." But this shallow and chauvinistic attitude of friends and relatives was perhaps fortunate for Emily Carr, conditioned by temperament to swim against the current. She had to struggle hard during the next fifteen years, earning her living by taking in boarders, raising and selling sheep dogs, pottery making, and rug-hooking. There was little or no time left for painting. Fortunately, Canadians in other parts of the country were working outside the conventional and fashionable stream of painting, and recognition of Emily Carr's paintings, particularly those of Indian subjects, came in 1927 when she was invited to exhibit fifty canvasses for a show of West Coast art at the National Gallery in Ottawa. It was during the exhibition which she attended that she had the opportunity to meet several members of the famous Group of Seven Canadian artists. Lawren Harris was particularly helpful to her, encouraging her in what she had accomplished, advising her in technique, and helping to give her the public recognition she deserved. She returned home with fresh vision and renewed vigor, survived many severe set-backs, and gradually won recognition both at home and in the United States.

But it is not only as an artist, and not primarily as an artist, that Emily Carr won wide recognition for her talents. Outside her native land, indeed, she is probably better known as a writer. Without grace or subtlety, her prose is distinguished simply because it expresses a mind of great integrity and character. What she says even about tri-

fles is memorable: "It was these tiny things, collec-
tively, taught me how to live. Too insignificant to
have been considered individually ... the little scraps
of nothingness of my life have made a definite pattern." The best of her writing is to be found in her
first book, Klee Wyck, a collection of short stories
describing her adventures among the Indian people.
It earned her the governor general's medal for non-
fiction in 1941. The sketches were written at various times, most often when she was seeking subjects
for her Indian canvasses in remote Indian villages
and forests. She is so clear-sighted and direct that
at times she startles: "In this place belonging neither to sea nor to land I came upon an old man
dressed in nothing but a brief shirt. He was sawing
the limbs from a fallen tree. The swish of the sea
tried to drown the purr of his saw. The purr of the
saw tried to sneak back into the forest, but the forest threw it out again into the sea. Sea and forest
were always at this game of toss with noises."
Emily and the old Indian had difficulty communicating
so in order to bridge the language barrier "we had
dumb talk, pointing to the sun and to the sea, the
eagles in the air and the crows on the beach. Nod-
ding and laughing together I sat and he sawed. The
old man sawed as if aeons of time were before him,
and as if all the years behind him had been leisurely
and all the years in front of him would be equally
free.... The shock of hair that fell to his shoulders
was grizzled. Life had sweetened the old man. He
was luscious with time like the end berries of the
strawberry season." It was her warm, impish mer-
riment in trying to communicate with the Indians that
earned her the name Klee Wyck, or "The Laughing
One."

Emily Carr had to struggle for everything, but
she had a few close friends and among them was a
CBC executive, Ira Dilworth, who discovered her as
a writer, edited several of her posthumously published books, wrote introductions to most of them
and became her literary executor. The story of
how she first came to be published is an interesting
one. It is told in a publisher's footnote to the limited edition of her journal: "It began one day in the
summer of 1940 when Ira Dilworth read aloud to W.

H. Clarke a manuscript which had been seen and
rejected by several publishing houses.   He read far
into the night and before morning the decision was
made: the material must be published immediately
and it must receive the very best production possible, as befitting the work of an outstanding new author. " In his introduction to Klee Wyck, Mr. Dilworth writes that Emily kept a notebook with her
when she painted in order to "word" her experience
because "this saying in words as well as in colour
and form gave me a double approach."   His introduction reflects the philosophy of her whole life as
a painter and a writer, her fierce insistence on
complete integrity, "do not write or paint anything
that is not your own"; her lyrical prose style, "the
song of the meadow-lark crumbled away the last
remnants of night, three sad lingering notes followed by an exultant double note that gobbled up
the still vibrating three"; and her firm belief that
the artist must speak clearly to the people, "she
was driven by a passion to make her own experience in the place in which life had set her vivid
and real for the on-looker or the reader and to
do it with dignity and distinction. "

FOREWORD BY IRA DILWORTH

to Emily Carr's
Klee Wyck

My earliest vivid memories of Emily Carr go back to
a period considerably more than a quarter of a century ago,
to a time when she was living in Victoria, British Columbia,
still largely unnoticed as an artist and, by most of those
who did know her in that capacity, unappreciated or treated
with ridicule and even hostility.   In those days she was a
familiar figure passing down Simcoe Street in front of our
house which was little more than a stone's throw away from
her home.   With methodical punctuality by which you could
almost have set your clock, she passed by each morning
on her way to the grocer's or butcher's.   She trundled in
front of her an old-fashioned baby carriage in which sat her
favourite pet, Woo, a small Javanese monkey dressed in a

bright costume of black, red and brown which Emily had
made for her. Bounding around her as she went would be
six or eight of the great shaggy sheep dogs which she raised
for sale. Half an hour later you could see her returning,
the baby carriage piled high with parcels, Woo skipping along
at the end of a leash, darting under the hedge to catch suc-
culent earwigs which she loved to crunch or sometimes creep-
ing right through the hedge into the garden to have her tail
pulled by the children hiding there. The great sheep dogs
still bounced around the quaint figure whom they recognized
as their devoted mistress. I thought of her then, as did the
children behind the hedge and as did most of her fellow-
citizens who thought of her at all, as an eccentric, middle-
aged woman who kept an apartment house on Simcoe Street
near Beacon Hill Park, who surrounded herself with numbers
of pets--birds, chipmunks, white rats and the favourite Woo--
and raised English sheep dogs in kennels in her large garden.

Emily Carr was a great painter, certainly one of the
greatest women painters of any time. It has been said that
for originality, versatility, driving creative power and
strong, individual achievement she has few equals among
modern artists. Her talent in drawing revealed itself when
she was still a small child and was encouraged by her father.
Emily set herself, early, and with singleness of devotion, to
master the technique of painting and, despite discouragement
and many difficulties, worked with great courage and experimental enthusiasm until the time of her death.

After the turn of the century, with study in San Francisco and England behind her, she became particularly concerned with the problem of devising a style in painting which
would make it possible for her to express adequately not only
what she saw but also what she felt in her subject matter--
the great totem poles, tribal houses and villages of the West
Coast Indians and, later, the tangled, solemn, majestic beauty of the Pacific Coast forest. Nothing ever meant so much
to her as the struggle to gain that power; she was never
satisfied that she had achieved her aim. In this connection,
therefore, it is interesting to have the opinion of Lawren
Harris, himself a great original Canadian painter and for
years one of Emily Carr's closest and most valued friends.
He says in an article, "The Paintings and Drawings of Emily
Carr, "

PRAISE FROM FAMOUS MEN

It [British Columbia] is another world from all the
land east of the Great Divide. Emily Carr was the
first artist to discover this. It involved her in a conscious struggle to achieve a technique that would
match the great, new motifs of British Columbia. It
was primarily this long and deepening discovery which
made her work modern and vital, as it was her love
of its moods, mystery and majesty that gave it the
quality of indwelling spirit which the Indians knew so
well. It was also her life with the Indians and their
native culture which led her to share and understand
their outlook on nature and life, and gave her paintings of totems, Indian villages and the forest a quality
and power which no white person had achieved before.

Emily Carr is now also recognized as a remarkable
writer. Her diaries, which first came to light after her
death and remain still unpublished, make it clear that her desire to express herself in words began in the late 1920's.
As in the case of her painting, she worked very hard to
master this medium. She was fascinated by the great range
of new possibilities which it opened up but mastery of it did
not come easily.

Why did she turn to writing? Sometimes, undoubtedly,
merely for comfort in her loneliness, sometimes quite con-
sciously to relive experiences of the past. She once told me
that when she was working on the first stages of a painting,
trying to put down in pictorial form a subject for which she
had made field sketches, she found it of great value to "word"
her experience. In this way, she said, the circumstances
and all the details of the incident or place would come back
to her more vividly and she could reconstruct them more
faithfully than was possible with paint and canvas alone.
From this developed, I suspect, one of the controlling principles of her method and style in literary composition.

I have seen her "peeling" a sentence, as she called
it, --a process which involved stripping away all ambiguous
or unnecessary words, replacing a vague word by a sharper,
clearer one until the sentence emerged clean and precise in
its meaning and strong in its impact on the reader. As a
result, there is in her writing the quality of immediacy, the
ability, by means of descriptive words chosen with the greatest accuracy, to carry the reader into the very heart of the

experience she is describing, whether it be an incident from
her own childhood or a sketch of an Indian and his village--
and that so swiftly as to give an impression almost of magic,
of incantation.

She has spoken many times in her diaries of the difficulties she had to overcome in writing.   Late in October,
1936, she made a characteristic, vivid entry:

> There's words enough, paint and brushes enough and
> thoughts enough.   The whole difficulty seems to be
> getting the thoughts clear enough, making them stand
> still long enough to be fitted with words and paint.
> They are so elusive--like wild birds singing above
> your head, twittering close beside you, chortling in
> front of you, but gone the moment you put out a hand.
> If ever you do catch hold of a piece of a thought it
> breaks away leaving the piece in your hand just to ag-
> gravate you.   If one only could encompass the whole,
> corral it, enclose it safe--but then maybe it would
> die, dwindle away because it could not go on growing.
> I don't think thoughts <u>could</u> stand still--the fringes of
> them would always be tangling into something just a
> little further on and that would draw it out and out.
> I guess that is just <u>why</u> it is so difficult to catch a
> complete idea--it's because everything is always on
> the move, always expanding.

A very closely related characteristic of her writing is
its sincerity.   I shall let her speak again for herself in her
own forceful, inimitable style.

> Be careful that you do not write or paint anything
> that is not your own, that you don't know in your own
> soul.   You will have to experiment and try things out
> for yourself and you will not be sure of what you are
> doing.   That's all right, you are feeling your way into
> the thing.   But don't take what someone else has made
> sure of and pretend that it's you yourself that have
> made sure of it, till it's yours absolutely by conviction.
> It's stealing to take it and hypocrisy and you'll fall in
> a hole....   If you're going to lick the icing off some-
> body else's cake you won't be nourished and it won't
> do you any good,--or you might find the cake had
> caraway seeds and you hate them.   But if you make

your own cake and <u>know</u> <u>the recipe and stir the thing</u>
<u>with your own hand</u> it's <u>your</u> own cake. You can ice
it or not as you like. Such lots of folks are licking
the icing off the other fellow's cake!

Consequently, Emily Carr's style is characterized by
a great simplicity and directness--a simplicity, it's true,
that is a little deceptive in view of the sustained discipline
from which it resulted--but perhaps it is just in that way
that the only true simplicity is achieved. Words are used by
her with great courage, sometimes taking on new and vivid
meanings. They are in her writing the equivalent of the
quick, sure brush strokes and dramatic, strong colours which
are so characteristic of her canvases.

It has been remarked by many readers--and with
justification--that Emily Carr's prose style has much in
common with poetry. This is to be seen in her rigid se-
lectivity in the use of diction described above, in her daring
use of metaphorical language, in the rhythm, the cadence of
her writing and in her consciousness of form. Look, for instance, at this passage from "Century Time":

> In the late afternoon a great shadow mountain stepped
> across the lake and brooded over the cemetery. It
> had done this at the end of every sunny day for cen-
> turies, long, long before that piece of land was a cem-
> etery. Dark came and held the shadow mountain there
> all night, but when morning broke, it was back again
> inside its mountain, which pushed its grand purple
> dome up into the sky and dared the pines swarming
> around its base to creep higher than half way up its
> bare rocky sides.
>   Indians do not hinder the progress of their dead by
> embalming or tight coffining. When the spirit has
> gone they give the body back to the earth. Cased
> only in a box it is laid in a shallow grave. The
> earth welcomes the body--coaxes new life and beauty
> from it, hurries over what men shudder at. Lovely
> tender herbage bursts from the graves--swiftly--
> exulting over corruption.

and again at this passage from "Bobtails":

> The top of Beacon Hill was bare. You could see

north, south, east and west. The dogs rested, tongues lolling, while I looked at the new day, at the pine trees, at the sky, at the sea where it lay flat, and at the near broom bushes drooped with early morning wetness. The song of the meadow-lark crumbled away the last remnants of night, three sad lingering notes followed by an exultant double note that gobbled up the still vibrating three.

For one moment the morning took you far out into vague chill; your body snatched you back into its cosiness, back to the waiting dogs on the hill top. They could not follow out there; their world was walled, their noses trailed the earth.

or at this from "Canoe":

The canoe passed shores crammed with trees, trees overhanging stony beaches, trees held back by rocky cliffs, pointed fir trees climbing its dark masses up the mountain sides, moonlight silvering their blackness.

Our going was imperceptible, the woman's steering paddle the only thing that moved, its silent cuts stirring phosphorus like white fire.

Time and texture faded, ceased to exist--day was gone, yet it was not night. Water was not wet or deep, just smoothness spread with light.

Such writing transcends the usual limits of prose and becomes (but without aesthetic offence) lyrical.

The quality of form, not a surprising attribute in view of her distinction as a painter, can be seen over and over again but notably in the exquisite lyric, "White Currants, " in the simply shaped but touchingly effective "Sophie" and in "D'Sonoqua" which has the quality of a musical symphony with its dominant themes, its sectional development and its use of suspense and tense emotional crescendo.

As a final point in this discussion of Emily Carr's literary style it should be noted that she was not a great reader. Her style is, therefore, not the result of imitation of literary models. Undoubtedly it is better so, for the originality and simplicity which marked all her work, whether in painting, rug-making, pottery or writing, remained uninhibited by academic literary standards. Of these Miss Carr knew little or nothing. But there is some literary influence. She was a devoted reader of the poems of Walt Whitman, attracted to them by Whitman's deep feeling for nature and by his vigorous style. There is too, I think, a discernible influence at times of the Bible, notably of the Psalms, and of the English Prayerbook.

But above everything else, Emily Carr was a truly great Canadian. Her devotion to her own land marked everything she did. She approached no subject in writing or painting with any condescension or purely artistic self-consciousness. She was driven always by a passion to make her own experience in the place in which life had set her vivid and real for the onlooker or the reader and to do this with dignity and distinction. She found life in her part of Canada often hard and baffling but always rich and full. It was her single purpose to share through the medium of her art and in as memorable a fashion as possible the experiences of her life. She was never happy outside Canada. Indeed, during her sojourns in England and France she was the victim of such overwhelming homesickness that she became physically ill and was ordered by her physician to return to her Canadian home.

She was an amazing woman. May I take the liberty of quoting a note which I set down in 1941? I hold the views as firmly today as then:

> I have heard her talking and watched her devour the conversation of others, of Lawren Harris, of Arthur Benjamin, of Garnett Sedgewick; I have watched her anger tower over some meanness in the work or conduct of an artist and I have seen her become incandescent with generous enthusiasm for another's fine work; I have seen her gentleness to an old woman and to an animal; I have beheld the vision of forest and sky enter and light her eyes as she sat far from them--and I am convinced that Emily Carr is a great genius and that we will do well to add her to that small list of originals who have been produced in this place and have lived and commented in one way or another on this Canada of ours.

Emily Carr was herself more modest. Asked a few

years before her death to state what had been the outstanding
events of her life, she wrote,

> Outstanding events!--work and more work! The most
> outstanding seems to me the buying of an old caravan
> trailer which I had towed to out-of-the-way corners
> and where I sat self-contained with dogs, monk and
> work--Walt Whitman and others on the shelf--writing
> in the long, dark evenings after painting--loving every-
> thing terrifically. In later years my work had some
> praise and some successes, but the outstanding event
> to me was the <u>doing</u> which I am still at. Don't pickle
> me away as a 'done.'

It is impossible to think of that vivid person as a
'done.' No, she goes on in her work. As surely as Wordsworth marked the English Lake District with his peculiar kind
of seeing and feeling, leaving us his experience patterned in
poetry, so surely this extraordinary, sensitive, gifted Canadian touched a part of our landscape and life and left her im-
print there so clearly that now we, who have seen her canvases or read her books must feel, as we enter the vastness
of the western forest or stand before a totem pole or in the
lonely ruin of an Indian village, less bewildered and alone
because we recognize that another was here before us and
humanized all this by setting down in paint or words her reaction to it.

IRA DILWORTH

Robin Hill,
Knowlton, P. Q.,
June, 1951

J. FRANK DOBIE

Born in 1859 in Indiana where his family owned a livestock farm, Andy Adams ran away from home to become a cowboy in Texas, and later settled in Colorado where he wrote his stories of the cattle kingdom. His most famous work, The Log of a Cowboy, published in 1903, is a picaresque novel about a five months' cattle drive in the late eighties from Brownsville, Texas, on the Mexican border, to the Blackfoot Agency on the Canadian border. Until the book was rescued from oblivion by J. Frank Dobie, Walter P. Webb, and others, it never received its just recognition from the American reading public, largely because Andy Adams portrays life among the cowboys and horses and cattle as it was lived rather than as it is presented in phoney TV versions and Zane Grey fantasies.

Cowboys are great people for talk around the chuckwagon and campfire and the yarns narrated in The Log through the voices of the cowboys are as old and simple and artful as an echo from Chaucer. "The stories may run from the sublime to the ridiculous," says Adams, "from a true incident to a base fabrication, or from a touching bit of pathos to the most vulgar vulgarity." They all have in common the cowmen and animals whose lives and actions have contributed to the narrator's understanding of life and added to his enjoyment: a saddle ox that could outswim any cowhorse; a sheepman mourning the rise in the price of coffee; a Scot known among the cowboys as the Professor because he knew so much about the stars; cattle drifting before a blizzard; stampedes and quicksand--these, and many more like them. In Frank Dobie's judgment The Log of the

J. FRANK DOBIE

Cowboy is "the best book that has ever been written
of cowboy life, and it is the best book that can ever
be written of cowboy life." That's a large order
but for those who are skeptical, there is the Dictionary of American Biography which regards it as
a minor classic, an "authentic portraiture of cowboy life in the days of the open range." For those
who like authentic westerns, it stands beside Bret
Harte's depiction of mining camps and the somber
hues of Hamsun's portrayal of Dakota pioneering
days.
      In his warm and friendly introduction to Andy
Adam's writings, printed in the Southwest Review,
J. Frank Dobie recalls some of the incidents in
the stories which he has most enjoyed, and he calls
particular attention to the author's honesty and quiet
naturalness, his gift of humor, and his use of picturesque language. Andy Adams would have responded modestly, as he did to another in his old
age: "My insight into cattle life was not obtained
from the window of a Pullman car, but close to the
soil and from the hurricane deck of a Texan horse.
Even today I am a better cowman than author, for
I can still rope and tie down a steer with any of
the boys, while in writing, the loop of the rope may
settle on the wrong foot of the rhetoric."

J. FRANK DOBIE

on "Andy Adams, Cowboy Chonicler"

      Five or six years ago I hunted all over San Antonio
for some books by Andy Adams, and I found just one. That
was one more than the Austin bookstores then had. A year
ago the proprietor of the largest book shop in Houston assured me that Andy Adams was out of print. Bookstores of
Oklahoma, Kansas, and Boston have proved as indifferent.
Happily, however, the apathy of some of the book dealers in
Texas, particularly in Austin and Dallas, has been overcome.
Now, thanks to an increasingly large number of individuals
who have insisted on the extraordinary merit of Andy Adams
as a writer and as a historian of the old-time cow people,

thousands of his books are being sold over the Southwest and his delayed fame is gaining over the entire country. Katharine Fullerton Gerould and Carl Van Doren have during the past year alluded to him. But the neglect is significant.

The histories of American literature have been singularly silent on him. A contributor to the Cambridge History of American Literature mentions him only to show that he has not read him. Boynton and Haney in their recent surveys of the field are silent; that considerate snapper-up of trifles, Fred Lewis Pattee, is silent. Several late authorities, however, mention in one way or another Harold Bell Wright and Zane Grey. Mr. Pattee quotes approvingly somebody's saying that Owen Wister's The Virginian is "our last glimpse of the pioneer plainsman and cowboy types, then passing and now gone." By "then" is, I suppose, meant the time at which The Virginian appeared; that was 1902. The Log of a Cowboy by Andy Adams, his first and perhaps best work, came out in 1903. Following it appeared A Texas Matchmaker (1904), The Outlet (1905), Cattle Brands (1906), Reed Anthony, Cowman (1907), and Wells Brothers--a book for "boys"--(1911).

The first four books are the best, perhaps, and I should rank them first, second, third, and fourth just as they appeared. Other readers disagree. The Log of a Cowboy is the best book that has ever been written of cowboy life, and it is the best book that ever can be written of cowboy life. With its complement, The Outlet, it gives a complete picture of trail cattle and trail drivers. Why has it been so overlooked by critics and historians?

In the first place, twenty years ago literary magazines and literary gentlemen were not concerning themselves with the cowboy. Occasionally an article on that subject got into polite print, but honest matter like Charlie Siringo's A Texas Cowboy was bound in paper and sold by butcher-boys-- a far cry from this day when the Yale University Press publishes James H. Cook's Fifty Years on the Old Frontier and then--with a Ph. D. preface--reprints Captain James B. Gillett's Six Years with the Texas Rangers. It is true that Owen Wister was at once accepted, but he went west as an Easterner and wrote of the cattle people not as one to the manner born but as a literary connoisseur. Even before him Frederic Remington with Pony Tracks and Crooked Trails

had been accepted into a well-deserved position that he has
never lost, but Remington was an artist to whom literature
was secondary and to whom the cowboy was tertiary in comparison with Indians and army men.   Remington also came
into the West looking for local color.

Andy Adams did not come into the cow country looking
for "copy."   Like Sam Bass, he "was born in Indiana," and
again like Sam Bass, "he first came out to Texas a cowboy
for to be."   He drove the trail as one of the hands.   He followed it very much as Conrad and Masefield followed the sea,
not as a writer but as a man of the element.   The miracle
is that when he did write he found such respectable publishers
as the Houghton Mifflin Company.   He now [1926] lives in
Colorado Springs, Colorado, aged sixty-six.

Of course, critics not only arouse interest but they
follow it, and Mr. Adams, in a letter, attributes neglect of
his books to the fact that he "could never make water run
uphill or use a fifth wheel," namely a girl.   But there is
another reason more paradoxical.   Generally the development
of a particular field by one writer creates a demand for the
works of other writers in the same milieu.   Unfortunately,
however, the demand for cowboy material was first aroused
by the "alkali Bill" type of writers; once aroused, that demand has never been satiated, and an avalanche of shoddy
has literally buried meritorious writing.   Could Andy Adams
have led the van, he might have become as well known in
his own field as Parkman became known in his.   Only just
now are responsible readers coming to wonder what the truth
about the cowboy is.   It is true that twenty years ago The
Log of a Cowboy was having something of a run and that the
newspapers were recording the usual indiscriminating banali-
ties that they record concerning any Western book, but the
present attempt at a serious review is just twenty-three
years late.

The great virtue of Andy Adams is fidelity, and The
Log of a Cowboy is a masterpiece for the same reason that
Two Years Before the Mast, Moby Dick, and Life on the
Mississippi are masterpieces.   All three of these chronicle-
records are of the water, and it is "symbolic of something,"
as Hawthorne would say, that the themes of three of the
most faithful expository narratives of America should be off-
shore.

Now the one part of America that has approached the sea in its length and breadth and dramatic solitude and its elemental power to overwhelm puny man has been the Great Plains. The one phase of American life that has approached the life of a ship's crew alone on the great deep battling the elements has been that of a cow outfit alone on the great trail that stretched across open ranges from Brownsville at the toe of the nation to northwestern Montana and on into Canada. All of Andy Adams's books treat of trail life, except one, A Texas Matchmaker, and it treats of ranch life in Southwest Texas during the trail-driving days. I have no hesitancy in saying that Mr. Adams has as truthfully and fully expressed the life of a trail outfit as Dana expressed the life of a crew that sailed around the Horn; that he is as warm in his sympathy for cowmen and horses and cattle as Mark Twain is in his feeling for pilots and the Mississippi River; and that he has treated of cattle as intimately and definitely, though not so scientifically or dramatically, as Melville treated of whales. Certainly, I have no idea of ranking Andy Adams as the equal of Mark Twain; I do not believe that he can be ranged alongside Herman Melville; but I should put him on an easy level with Richard Henry Dana, Jr. The immense importance of his subject to the western half of the United States makes him in a way more important historically than either Melville or Dana.

Andy Adams has a racy sympathy for the land and for the cattle and horses and men of the land. He savors them deep, but he savors them quietly. Sometimes there are storms and stampedes, but generally the herds just "mosey along." Cattle bog in the quicksands and there is desperate work to pull them out, but oftener they graze in the sunshine and chew their cuds by still waters while the owner rides among them from sheer love of seeing their contentment and thriftiness. One old Texas steer took so much pleasure in hearing the Confederate boys sing "Rock of Ages" that they could not bear to slaughter him. One trail outfit made a great pet of a calf, and for hundreds of miles it followed the chuckwagon, much to the exasperation of its mother. On another trip there was a certain muley steer that the horned cattle hooked, and at night the boys used to let him wander out of the herd to lie down in a private bed. One spring Reed Anthony, the great cowman, could not find it in his heart to order a roundup because "chousing" the cattle would disturb the little calves "playing in groups" and "lying like

fawns in the tall grass." "The Story of a Poker Steer" in
Cattle Brands is a classic; its delineation of the life of a
"linebacked calf" is as quiet and easy as Kipling's "Story of
the White Seal." Tom Quirk, boarding a train in Montana,
thousands of miles away from his Texas home, was grieved
indeed to part from his saddle horse forever.

No matter whether the theme is a pet calf or a terrible "die-up" in "the Territory," there is absolutely no strain
in Andy Adams. This quality of reserve distinguishes him
from all other Western writers that I know of. One can but
contrast him with the Zane Grey school so ubiquitously ex-
ploited by nearly every American institution ranging from a
two-bit drugstore to Harper and Brothers. In Zane Grey's
U. P. Trail, for instance, which has often been hailed as a
piece of real history, the men "were grim; they were in-
domitable"; and the heroine "clutched Neal with fingers of
steel, in a grip that he could not have loosened without
breaking her bones."

Not long ago a friend was telling me of an incident
so expressive that I must repeat it. This friend was camp-
ing in a canyon out in Arizona, where he was excavating
some Indian ruins. One night he was awakened by unearthly
yelling and shooting and the clatter of horses' hoofs. Rush-
ing out of his tent, he met a cowboy whom he knew. "What
is the matter?" he asked. "Oh," replied the cowboy,
"there's a feller coming back yonder who hired us to give
him some local color, as he calls it. His name's Zane
Grey, and we're doing our damndest to give him all the hell
he calls for."

Now in Andy Adams always "there is ample time,"
as he makes "a true Texan" say. To quote the words of
Gilbert Chesterton on Sir Walter Scott's heroes, "the men
linger long at their meals." Indeed, I think that the best
things in the books of Mr. Adams are the tales that the men
tell around the chuckwagon and the jokes and the chaff that
they indulge in there.

An easy intimacy with the life shows on every page.
The man writes of the only life he knows, in the only language he knows. "Now, Miller, the foreman, hadn't any
use for a man that wasn't dead tough under any condition.
I've known him to camp his outfit on alkali water, so the

men would get out in the morning, and every rascal beg leave to ride outside circle on the morning round-up. " "Cattle will not graze freely in a heavy dew or too early in the morning. " When Don Lovell's outfit received a herd of cattle on the Rio Grande, the Texas boss tallied the hundreds with a tally string and the Mexican caporal tallied them by dropping pebbles from one hand to the other. When June Deweese, segundo, showed off his boss's horses to a buyer below San Antonio, he had them grazing on a hillside and drove the buyer along on the lower slope so that they would appear larger.

The language that the Andy Adams cowboys use is as natural and honest as the exposition; it is often picturesque, too, as all language of the soil is. I quote sentences almost at random from various of the books. "I'll build a fire in your face that you can read the San Francisco 'Examiner' by at midnight. " "We had the outfits and the horses, and our men were plainsmen and were at home as long as they could see the north star. " "The old lady was bogged to the saddle skirts in her story. " "Blankets? Never use them; sleep on your belly and cover with your back, and get up with the birds in the morning. " "Every good cowman takes his saddle wherever he goes, though he may not have clothes enough to dust a fiddle. "

A year or so ago in a senseless attack on the historical accuracy of Emerson Hough's North of Thirty-Six, Stuart Henry said that the Texans who reached Abilene in 1867 did not celebrate the Fourth of July. The charge, along with others, was repudiated by some good Texas Americans. Now, as a matter of fact, it is very likely that the Texans of 1867 did not celebrate the Fourth of July in Abilene or anywhere else. I know a few--and they are out of the old rock, too--who still pay more attention to April 21 than to July 4. During the three decades following the Civil War more than ten millions of cattle were trailed north from Texas; they were trailed across every river and into every range of the West, and wherever they were trailed the pointmen were Texans. Generally those Texans were either Confederate soldiers or the sons of Confederate soldiers. Andy Adams has been very careful to catch the temper of those Texans fresh from the ranks of the Confederate Army. He has not allowed, like other writers, a mushy patriotism to abnegate the justified pride of a section, though in his books the halest of partnerships are formed between "rebels" and

Yankees. In 1882, at Frenchman's Ford on the Yellowstone,
"The Rebel, " a memorable hand in The Log of a Cowboy,
exulted over a "patriotic beauty" with a toast that went thus:
"Jeff Davis and the Southern Confederacy. "

When I began reading Andy Adams a number of years
ago, the humor of his books did not impress me. Lately I
have found it to be one of their highest virtues. Folk yarns
salt page after page, and many a good-natured drawl sets me
laughing. The humor is as unconscious as the green of
grass, but I do not know of anything in Mark Twain funnier
than the long story of the "chuckline rider" who blew into a
cow camp in "The Strip" about Christmas time and proceeded
to earn his board by cooking "bear sign" (the name for dough-
nuts). The cowboys often play like colts; one of them gets
down off his horse and butts his head into a muddy bank,
imitative of the cattle; some of them dress up one of their
number like a wild Indian and take him to the hotel for dinner. This is horseplay, to be sure, but as it is told it gen-
erates health in a healthy reader like a good feed of roast
beef and plum pudding.

There are, of course, many shortcomings in Mr.
Adams. His books have no plots, but lack of plot sometimes
allows of an easier fidelity to facts. He lacks great dramatic
power, unless the quiet truth be dramatic. However, there is
plenty of action on occasion. "The men of that day, " says the
author of Reed Anthony, Cowman, which like all the other
novels but one is written in the autobiographic style, "were
willing to back their opinions, even on trivial matters, with
their lives. 'I'm the quickest man on the trigger that ever
came over the trail, ' said a cow puncher to me one night in
a saloon in Abilene. 'You're a blankety blank liar, ' said a
quiet little man, a perfect stranger to both of us, not even
casting a glance our way. I wrested a six-shooter from the
hands of my acquaintance, and hustled him out of the house,
getting roundly cursed for my interference, though no doubt
I saved human life. "

The greatest shortcoming, perhaps, is too much love
of prosperity. Andy Adams loves cowmen and cattle and
horses so that he can hardly suffer any of them to undergo
ruin. The trail has hardships, but it is delightful. The
path of the owner and his cowboys is sometimes rocky, but
it generally leads down into pleasant pastures. As they trav-

el it, they never go into heroics about their "grim sacrifices,"
etc.; they take great gusto in the traveling.   When I read
Reed Anthony, Cowman or Wells Brothers, I think of old
Daniel Defoe's love for goods of the earth, and I would no
more think of holding their prosperity against the actuality of
Reed Anthony, Don Lovell, and other prosperous cattle people of Andy Adams's creation than I would think of impeach-
ing the life-likeness of Mulberry Sellers on account of his
optimism.

There are no women in Andy Adams, excepting those
in the melancholy Matchmaker.   Well, there were no women
in the action that he treats of.   Why should he lug them in?
Nor has Andy Adams any thesis to advance.   He has no absorbing philosophy of life that mingles with the dark elements
of earth as in Joseph Conrad.   "To those who love them,
cattle and horses are good company."   Perhaps that is his
philosophy.

It is easy to let one's enthusiasm run away with one's
judgment.   I have waited a long time to write these words
on Andy Adams.   Perhaps sympathy for his subject has biased
me.   Perhaps the memory of how a dear uncle of mine used
to "run" with him at the end of the trail in Caldwell, Kansas,
has affected me.   I try to rule those elements out.   It is my
firm conviction that one hundred, three hundred years from
now people will read Andy Adams to see what the life of
those men who went up the trail from Texas was like, just
as we now read the diary of Pepys to see what life in London was like following the Restoration, or as we read the
Spectator papers to see what it was like in the Augustan age.
Those readers of other centuries will miss in Andy Adams
the fine art of Addison, though they will find something of
the same serenity; they will miss the complex character and
debonair judgments of Pepys; but they will find the honesty
and fidelity of a man who rode his horses straight without
giving them the sore-back and then who traced his trail so
plainly that even a tenderfoot may follow it without getting
lost.

The Greeks liked their stories raw and violent
and got what they wanted from Euripides in the child-
murder of Medea. The civilized Englishman prefers his violence in parables and gets what he wants
from accounts of savage-civilized children as set
forth in the novels of Richard Hughes and William
Golding.

In 1929 Richard Hughes startled the literary
world with the publication in England and America
of his novel The Innocent Voyage, retitled the following year A High Wind in Jamaica, which begins
as a Stevensonian yarn and ends in terror. In 1954
William Golding came out with his willful, wayward
novel, entitled Lord of the Flies, which tells the
story of a group of young children, stranded on an
island, whose conduct gradually recedes from the
normal of English schoolboys individually to that of
the pitiless, implacable savagery of the mob. The
novel is an extraordinary mixture: the initial effort
of normal, innocent kids, sole survivors of an air-
crash, striving to organize themselves and keep sig-
nals burning until rescued; the swath cut by leaders
of different temperaments through the actions of the
boys; the lurking menace of the "Thing" or "Beast"
which scares hell out of the children, but which in
reality is a dead airman whose parachute and har-
ness sway grotesquely in the wind from the highest
point on the island; the dissolving effect of fear of
the unknown on the conduct of the children; evil
bursting forth nakedly in the murder of two boys and
the hunting down of the leader who tries to hold the
group to some standard of decency. All is told in
a swiftly paced narrative as exciting as it is chilling.

PRAISE FROM FAMOUS MEN

These two novels are no simple adventure stories of children on a voyage or desert island. The children are figures in a parable or fable, as E. P. Epstein points out in his afterword to Lord of the Flies. A similar theme is to be found in Christopher Morley's Thunder on the Left which begins realistically with a children's birthday party, after which the children are, by some strange magic, projected into maturity where they spy on one another and experience the very realistic unhappiness that awaits them. The connective theme that develops from all three novels is what the human condition is all about, and what human life amounts to.

NOTES BY E. L. EPSTEIN

on William Golding's
Lord of the Flies

In answer to a publicity questionnaire from the American publishers of Lord of the Flies, William Golding (born Cornwall, 1911) declared that he was brought up to be a scientist, and revolted; after two years of Oxford he changed his educational emphasis from science to English literature, and became devoted to Anglo-Saxon. After publishing a volume of poetry he "wasted the next four years," and when World War II broke out he joined the Royal Navy. For the next five years he was involved in naval matters except for a few months in New York and six months with Lord Cherwell in a "research establishment." He finished his naval career as a Lieutenant in command of a rocket ship; he had seen action against battleships, submarines and aircraft, and had participated in the Walcheren and D-Day operations. After the war he began teaching and writing. Today, his novels include Lord of the Flies (Coward-McCann), The Inheritors (which may loosely be described as a novel of prehistory but is, like all of Golding's work, much more), and Pincher Martin (Capricorn 66; pub. in hardcover by Harcourt Brace as The Two Deaths of Christopher Martin). He lists his Hobbies as thinking, classical Greek, sailing and archaeology, and his Literary Influences as Euripides and the anonymous Anglo-Saxon author of The Battle of Maldon.

E. L. EPSTEIN

The theme of Lord of the Flies is described by Golding as follows (in the same publicity questionnaire): "The theme is an attempt to trace the defects of society back to the defects of human nature. The moral is that the shape of a society must depend on the ethical nature of the individual and not on any political system however apparently logical or respectable. The whole book is symbolic in nature except the rescue in the end where adult life appears, dignified and capable, but in reality enmeshed in the same evil as the symbolic life of the children on the island. The officer, having interrupted a man-hunt, prepares to take the children off the island in a cruiser which will presently be hunting its enemy in the same implacable way. And who will rescue the adult and his cruiser?"

This is, of course, merely a casual summing-up on Mr. Golding's part of his extremely complex and beautifully woven symbolic web which becomes apparent as we follow through the book, but it does indicate that Lord of the Flies is not, to say the least, a simple adventure story of boys on a desert island. In fact, the implications of the story go far beyond the degeneration of a few children. What is unique about the work of Golding is the way he has combined and synthesized all of the characteristically twentieth-century methods of analysis of the human being and human society and used this unified knowledge to comment on a "test situation." In this book, as in few others at the present time, are findings of psychoanalysts of all schools, anthropologists, social psychologists and philosophical historians mobilized into an attack upon the central problem of modern thought: the nature of the human personality and the reflection of personality on society.

Another feature of Golding's work is the superb use of symbolism, a symbolism that "works." The central symbol itself, the "lord of the flies," is, like any true symbol, much more than the sum of its parts; but some elements of it may be isolated. The "lord of the flies" is a translation of the Hebrew Ba'alzevuo (Beelzebub in Greek). It has been suggested that is was a mistranslation of a mistransliterated word which gave us this pungent and suggestive name for the Devil, a devil whose name suggests that he is devoted to decay, destruction, demoralization, hysteria and panic and who therefore fits in very well with Golding's theme.

The Devil is not present in any traditional religious sense; Golding's Beelzebub is the modern equivalent, the anarchic, amoral, driving force that Freudians call the Id, whose only function seems to be to insure the survival of the host in which it is embedded or embodied, which function it performs with tremendous and single-minded tenacity. Although it is possible to find other names for this force, the modern picture of the personality, whether drawn by theologians or psychoanalysts, inevitably includes this force or psychic structure as the fundamental principle of the Natural Man. The tenets of civilization, the moral and social codes, the Ego, the intelligence itself, form only a veneer over this white-hot power, this uncontrollable force, "the fury and the mire of human veins." Dostoievsky found salvation in this freedom, although he found damnation in it also. Yeats found in it the only source of creative genius ("Whatever flames upon the night, / Man's own resinous heart has fed."). Conrad was appalled by this "heart of darkness," and existentialists find in the denial of this freedom the source of perversion of all human values. Indeed one could, if one were so minded, go through the entire canon of modern literature, philosophy and psychology and find this great basic drive defined as underlying the most fundamental conclusions of modern thought.

The emergence of this concealed, basic wildness is the theme of the book; the struggle between Ralph, the representative of civilization with his parliaments and his brain trust (Piggy, the intellectual whose shattering spectacles mark the progressive decay of rational influence as the story progresses), and Jack, in whom the spark of wildness burns hotter and closer to the surface than in Ralph and who is the leader of the forces of anarchy on the island, is also, of course, the struggle in modern society between those same forces translated onto a worldwide scale.

The turning point in the struggle between Ralph and Jack is the killing of the sow (pp. 124-133). The sow is a mother: "sunk in deep maternal bliss lay the largest of the lot ... the great bladder of her belly was fringed with a row of piglets that slept or burrowed and squeaked." The killing of the sow is accomplished in terms of sexual intercourse.

They were just behind her when she staggered into an open space where bright flowers grew and butter-

flies danced round each other and the air was hot and
still.

Here, struck down by the heat, the sow fell and
the hunters hurled themselves at her. This dreadful
eruption from an unknown world made her frantic;
she squealed and bucked and the air was full of sweat
and noise and blood and terror. Roger ran round the
heap, prodding with his spear whenever pigflesh appeared. Jack was on top of the sow, stabbing downward with his knife. Roger [a natural sadist, who
becomes the 'official' torturer and executioner for the
tribe] found a lodgment for his point and began to
push till he was leaning with his whole weight. The
spear moved forward inch by inch, and the terrified
squealing became a high-pitched scream. Then Jack
found the throat and the hot blood spouted over his
hands. The sow collapsed under them and they were
heavy and fulfilled upon her. The butterflies still
danced, preoccupied in the center of the clearing.

The pig's head is cut off; a stick is sharpened at both ends
and "jammed in a crack" in the earth. (The death planned
for Ralph at the end of the book involves a stick sharpened
at both ends.) The pig's head is impaled on the stick; "...
the head hung there, a little blood dribbling down the stick.
Instinctively the boys drew back too; and the forest was very
still. They listened, and the loudest noise was the buzzing
of flies over the spilled guts." Jack offers this grotesque
trophy to "the Beast," the terrible animal that the littler
children had been dreaming of, and which seems to be lurking on the island wherever they were not looking. The entire incident forms a horrid parody of an Oedipal wedding
night; these emotions, the sensations aroused by murder and
death, and the overpowering and unaccustomed emotions of
sexual love experienced by the half-grown boys, plus their
own irrational fears and blind terrors, release the forces
of death and the devil on the island.

After this occurs the most deeply symbolic incident
in the book, the "interview" of Simon, an embryo mystic,
with the head. The head seems to be saying, to Simon's
heightened perceptions, that "everything was a bad business.... The half-shut eyes were dim with the infinite
cynicism of adult life." Simon fights with all his feeble
power against the message of the head, against the "ancient,

inescapable recognition, " the recognition of human capacities
for evil and the superficial nature of human moral systems.
It is the knowledge of the end of innocence, for which Ralph
is to weep at the close of the book. " 'Fancy thinking the
Beast was something you could hunt and kill' said the head.
For a moment or two the forest and all the other dimly appreciated places echoed with the parody of laughter. 'You
knew, didn't you? I'm part of you? Close, close, close!
I'm the reason why it's no go? Why things are what they
are?' "

At the end of this fantastic scene Simon imagines he
is looking into a vast mouth. "There was blackness within,
a blackness that spread.... Simon was inside the mouth.
He fell down and lost consciousness." This mouth, the symbol of ravenous, unreasoning and eternally insatiable nature,
appears again in Pincher Martin, in which the development
of the theme of a Nature inimical to the conscious personality of man is developed in a stunning fashion. In Lord of
the Flies, however, only the outline of a philosophy is
sketched, and the boys of the island are figures in a parable
or fable which like all great parables or fables reveals to
the reader an intimate, disquieting connection between the innocent, time-passing, story-telling aspect of its surface and
the great, "dimly appreciated" depths of its interior.

E. L. Epstein

MORRIS L. ERNST

From the very beginning, books have drawn the fire of censors and it seems more than likely that there will always be those who continue to work overtime in an effort to suppress what they are against. Morris Ernst, on the other hand, was a valiant champion in defense of book freedom and his handling of the legal fight which made possible the publication of James Joyce's Ulysses in this country is no doubt the highlight of his long and distinguished career in the cause of enlightenment.

The Ulysses case was tried before the United States District Court of New York and the decision was rendered December 6, 1933. Judge John M. Woolsey, the presiding judge, wrote the opinion permitting the publication of Ulysses in the United States. In an appreciative introduction to the first American edition of Ulysses, published shortly after the decision, Ernst salutes Judge Woolsey as a "master of juridical prose" and credits him with having "charted a labyrinthine branch of the law."

The formula laid down by the court to determine what was censorable stressed the literary merit of the work, the author's intent, and the necessity for judging the work as a whole rather than any part or words in isolation. Ernst, and others opposed to censorship, expressed the hope that Judge Woolsey's decision would henceforth terminate all external controls on literary publication and reading, but this has not proved to be the case. Freedom to read is never assured in this contingent world. Stupidity, changes in taste, the difficulty of defining pornography in terms that make sense, and the widespread distribution of real hard-core stuff--these are some of the hazards to a solution of the problem. The 1973 Supreme Court ruling which gave individual states and local communities the right to ban books offered no solution. It merely substituted a multiplicity of variable community standards for national guidelines. We take for granted, of course, that we are free to speak and read as we wish, protesting in Elmer Davis's words but we were born free. So we were, but that freedom can be retained "only by eternal vigilance which has always been its price." In practical effect what happens under existing law depends largely upon how much pressure can be brought on local officials by the demands of a vociferous few. Therefore it is more important than ever before that people in a community representing all sides of a question of censorship stand up and make their views known.

FOREWORD BY MORRIS L. ERNST

to James Joyce's
Ulysses

The New Deal in the law of letters is here. Judge Woolsey has exonerated Ulysses of the charge of obscenity, handing down an opinion that bids fair to become a major event in the history of the struggle for free expression. Joyce's masterpiece, for the circulation of which people have been branded criminals in the past, may now freely enter this country.

It would be difficult to overestimate the importance of Judge Woolsey's decision. For decades the censors have fought to emasculate literature. They have tried to set up the sensibilities of the prudery-ridden as a criterion for society, have sought to reduce the reading matter of adults to the level of adolescents and subnormal persons, and have nurtured evasions and sanctimonies.

The Ulysses case marks a turning point. It is a body-blow for the censors. The necessity for hypocrisy and circumlocution in literature has been eliminated. Writers need no longer seek refuge in euphemisms. They may now describe basic human functions without fear of the law.

The Ulysses case has a three-fold significance. The
definition and criteria of obscenity have long vexed us.
Judge Woolsey has given us a formula which is lucid, rational and practical. In doing so he has not only charted a
labyrinthine branch of the law, but has written an opinion
which raises him to the level of former Supreme Court Justice Oliver Wendell Holmes as a master of juridical prose.
His service to the cause of free letters has been of no lesser
moment. But perhaps his greatest service has been to the
community. The precedent he has established will do much
to rescue the mental pabulum of the public from the censors
who have striven to convert it into treacle, and will help to
make it the strong, provocative fare it ought to be.

The first week of December 1933 will go down in history for two repeals, that of Prohibition and that of the legal
compulsion for squeamishness in literature. It is not incon-
ceivable that these two have been closely interlinked in the
recent past, and that sex repressions found vent in intem-
perance. At any rate, we may now imbibe freely of the contents of bottles and forthright books. It may well be that in
the future the repeal of the sex taboo in letters will prove to
be of the greater importance. Perhaps the intolerance which
closed our distilleries was the intolerance which decreed that
basic human functions had to be treated in books in a furtive,
leering, roundabout manner. Happily, both of these have
now been repudiated.

The Ulysses case is the culmination of a protracted
and stubborn struggle against the censors dating back to the
victory over the New York Vice Society in the Mademoiselle
de Maupin case in 1922. Coming in logical sequence after
the Well of Loneliness case, the Dennett case, the cases in-
volving Dr. Stopes' books, the Casanova's Homecoming case,
the Frankie and Johnnie case, and the God's Little Acre case,
all of which have served to liberalize the law of obscenity,
the victory of Ulysses is a fitting climax to the salutary forward march of our courts.

Under the Ulysses case it should henceforth be impossible for the censors legally to sustain an attack against any
book of artistic integrity, no matter how frank and forthright
it may be. We have travelled a long way from the days of

Bowdler and Mrs. Grundy and Comstock. We may well rejoice over the result.

MORRIS L. ERNST

New York, December 11, 1933

E. M. FORSTER

Maurice O'Sullivan's <u>Twenty Years A-Growing</u> is unique--a very odd document, Forster calls it in a sympathetic introduction--but thoroughly enjoyable even if descriptions of childhood days in the Blasket Islands off the coast of Ireland do not unduly attract the reader. Threaded on the story of the boy's life are chapters describing his memories of every aspect of life on the island on which he lived--a first day at school, fishing and hunting, rounding up the sheep, hunting thrushes in the dark of Hallowe'en, match-making, a wedding, and a wake. Land is scarce but somehow the islanders manage. They bake their daily bread. They build their own houses. They make their curraghs--and their coffins. They sing, they laugh, they drink, and they pray. If ever there was a lesson in courage, these people could teach it by example. But O'Sullivan gives no hint of austerity, of the inclemency of wind and rain, and of the lack of comforts. For him the Great Blasket is a summer island of romantic beauty where the old men are full of wise sayings, the old women gossip and puff on their pipes, and the young men fish, hunt, and dance with beautiful partners. Toward the end of his autobiography, he describes how he left his native home and went to Dublin where he joined the Irish police force.

<u>Twenty Years A-Growing</u> was written in Irish, translated into English by Moya L. Davies and George Thomson, whose qualifications and skill are prominently mentioned by Forster in his introduction, and published in 1933. The translators state in their own preface that it is "the first translation into English of a genuine account of the life of the Irish

peasants written by one of themselves, as distinct
from what has been written about them by the poets
and dramatists of the Anglo-Irish school. "

INTRODUCTORY NOTE BY E. M. FORSTER

to Maurice O'Sullivan's
Twenty Years A-Growing

The best introduction to this autobiography is its own
first chapter. If the reader laughs at the schoolmistress
and the matrons, and is moved by the dream of the butterfly
inside the horse's skull--then he is assured of amusement
and emotion to come. He is ready to go on to Ventry Races,
and to make the great journey from Dingle east, where O'Con-
nor and the girl were so unreliable. He is ready, furthermore, to make another journey: to steal out on Hallowe'en
and catch thrushes above waves of the living and the dead,
and see the Land of the Young in the west, and hear the
mother-seal saying to the hunter, "If you are in luck you
will leave this cove in haste, for be it known to you that you
will not easily kill my young son. " All this--both the gaiety
and the magic--can be sampled in the opening chapter, and
the reader can decide for himself quickly, so that there is
no need to say to him "This book is good. "

But it is worth saying "This book is unique, " lest he
forget what a very odd document he has got hold of. He is
about to read an account of neolithic civilization from the inside. Synge and others have described it from the outside,
and very sympathetically, but I know of no other instance
where it has itself become vocal, and addressed modernity.
Nor is a wiseacre speaking for it; we are entertained by a
lively young man, who likes dancing and the movies, and was
smart at his lessons. But he is able to keep our world in
its place, and to view it only from his own place, and his
spirit never abandons the stronghold to which, in the final
chapter, his feet will return. "When I returned home, the
lamps were being lit in the houses. I went in. My father
and grandfather were sitting on either side of the fire, my
grandfather smoking his old pipe. " With these words the
story closes, and it is as if a shutter descends behind which
all three generations disappear, and their Island with them.

The book is written in Irish, and the original is being published in Dublin. As regards the translators, one of them is in close and delicate touch with the instincts of her country-side, the other, a scholar, teaches Greek through the medium of Irish in the University of Galway. I know the author, too. He is now in the Civic Guard in Connemara, and though he is pleased that his book should be translated, his main care is for the Irish original, because it will be read on the Blasket. They will appreciate it there more than we can, for whom the wit and poetry must be veiled. On the other hand, we are their superiors in astonishment. They cannot possibly be as much surprised as we are, for here is the egg of a sea-bird--lovely, perfect, and laid this very morning.

E. M. FORSTER

If the intelligent reader has been uneasily aware for sometime of the need to grapple with the basic concepts of Freudian theory, and has been unsuccessful so far, a fascinating book entitled Ritual: Psycho-analytic Studies may offer a good opening hold. The author was a German analyst, Dr. Theodor Reik, and his book, first published in German in 1919, was translated by Douglas Bryan, from the second German edition, in 1946. Reik's studies have been rather precisely defined by William Maxwell in the New York Times Book Review as "psychological detective stories." The comparison is an apt one. The principal characters are from different backgrounds, the facts are startling enough, and the author is a master of fluent prose.

Ritual is based on a hypothesis, first promulgated by Sigmund Freud in Totem and Taboo, that views ceremonial as revolving about the father-son relationship. The author then proceeds, by the accumulation and collation of data and by analogies among innumerable details, to the exploration of these facts and details in accordance with psychoanalytic technique. The victim in the four studies is identified by Freud in his preface to Ritual: "... god the father at one time walked incarnate on the earth and exercised his sovereignty as leader of the hordes of primitive men until his sons combined together and slew him; ... the first social ties, the basic moral restrictions, and the oldest form of religion--totemism--originated as a result of, and a reaction against, this liberating misdeed."

At the base of each of his four studies of religious ritual, Reik finds the stirrings of this ancient

crime of parricide. In the first, the couvade or
male child-bed, he describes the fasting and puri-
fication of the father when a child is born and as-
cribes couvade practices to the motive of expiation
for the father's hostile wishes toward his own father, in order to avert retaliation from his sons.
In the second, which relates to puberty rites among
certain primitive societies in Australia, the father
again satisfies his hate and fear of his growing sons
through a totem monster who requires their circum-
cision, after which they are reborn, reconciled with
the father, and formally accepted into the tribe.
The third study explains the ancient Jewish custom
of the Kol Nidre (apparently invalidating future oaths)
as a repetition of the original parricide and atone-
ment for it. The final study, the blowing of the
shofar or ram's horn, is interpreted as a triumphant
identification with the divine voice as well as a rec-
onciliation with the slain and worshiped father.

In these studies Reik is concerned only with the
psychological origins of ceremonial and the psychic
paths taken in its development. He recognizes that
there are many approaches to the study of religious
phenomena and that the method of psychoanalysis is
only one of them, albeit an important one. "In in-
vestigating the problems of religion," he writes, "we
are obliged constantly to keep in mind the unconscious processes; otherwise we are in great danger
of building an edifice that will be blown down at the
first breath of wind." By considering the details of
primitive religious life in accordance with psycho-
analytic technique, he hopes to throw light upon the
"fundamental presuppositions and ultimate aims of
religion."

In his introduction to Ritual, Freud not only sets
the stage for Reik's studies of ceremonial but also
provides an admirably clear account (he was at one
time awarded the Goethe medal for style in scientific writing) of the origin and method of psycho-
analysis. An important and somewhat startling
phase of his research is touched on in the preface
when he asserts that "individual forms of neuroses
show a marked correspondence with the most highly
valued products of our civilization." In short, the
mentally deranged are "making, in an asocial man-

ner, the same attempts at a solution of their conflicts and an appeasement of their urgent desires which, when carried out in a manner acceptable to a large number of persons, are called poetry, religion, and philosophy. " Think that over! The impact is likely to linger.

Most of the downpour of books about Freud and psychoanalysis are written from a partisan point of view. Professor Hanns Sach places him in a class with Shakespeare and Galileo among the world's four or five great geniuses, but Sachs was a disciple and intimate. If the forbidding size of the canonical writings (The Standard Edition of the Complete Psychological Works of Sigmund Freud, edited by James Strachey, 24 volumes) puts you off, there are the highly selective Basic Writings of Sigmund Freud, translated and edited by A. A. Brill, and the more extensive selections of the master's writings in the Pelican Freud Library paperbacks, edited by James Strachey and Angelo Richards.

PREFACE BY SIGMUND FREUD

to Theodor Reik's
Ritual: Psycho-analytic Studies

Psycho-analysis was born of medical necessity. It originated in the need of helping the victims of nervous disease to whom rest, hydropathy or electrical treatment could bring no relief. A striking case recorded by Joseph Breuer had aroused the hope that the amount of help that could be given to such patients might vary directly with the extent to which it might be possible to understand the genesis, hitherto unfathomed, of their symptoms. Psycho-analysis, therefore, though originally a matter of purely medical technique, was directed, from the first, towards new research, towards the discovery of mechanisms whose nature was concealed but whose effects were far-reaching.

Its further progress led away from the study of the physical conditions of nervous illnesses in a degree surprising to the physician, and gradually the whole mental content of human life came within its sphere, including the healthy--the normal as well as the super-normal. It had to concern itself with affects and passions, and above all, with those constant subjects of the poet's art and enthusiasm, the emotions of love: it learnt to recognise the potency of memories, the unsuspected significance of the early years of childhood in shaping the conduct of later life, and finally the strength of those wishes which lead men's judgements astray and prescribe the paths of human endeavour.

For a time it appeared to be the fate of psychoanalysis to be incorporated into the field of psychology without being able to indicate in what way the mind of the sick patient differed from that of the normal person. But in the course of its development it came upon the problem of the dream, which is an abnormal mental product created by normal people under regularly recurring physiological conditions. And in solving the enigma of dreams it found in unconscious mentality the common ground in which the highest as well as the lowest mental impulses are rooted, and from which arise the most normal mental activities as well as the strange products of a diseased mind. The picture of the mental mechanisms of the individual now became clearer and more complete: it was seen that obscure impulses arising in his organic life were striving to fulfil their own aims, and that controlling them was a series of more highly organised mental formations, acquired and handed on by man under the pressure of his cultural development, which had taken possession of parts of these impulses, developed them or employed them in the service of higher aims--had bound them fast, at all events, and utilised their energy for its own purposes. This higher organisation, which we know as the ego, had rejected another portion of the same elementary impulses as useless, because these impulses could not accommodate themselves to the organic unity of the individual, or because they conflicted with its cultural aims. The ego was not powerful enough to exterminate those mental forces it could not control. Instead, it turned away from them, leaving them on the most primitive psychological level, and protected itself against their demands by means of energetic defensive or reactive mechanisms, or sought to compromise with them by means of substitute-gratifications. Unsubdued and indestructible, yet inhibited in every direction, these repressed impulses, together with their primitive mental content, form the underworld, the kernel of the true unconscious, ever on the alert to urge their claims and to find

any means for gratification.   Hence the insecurity of our
proud psychical superstructure, the nightly emergence of
proscribed and repressed things in dreams, and our prone-
ness to fall ill with neuroses and psychoses as soon as the
distribution of power between the ego and the repressed is
altered to the disadvantage of the former.

It requires but little consideration to realise that such
a view of the life of the human mind cannot possibly be limited to the sphere of dreams and nervous diseases.   If it be
a justifiable view, it must apply also to normal mental phenomena, and even the highest achievements of the human mind
must have some relation to the factors recognised in path-
ology--to repression, to the strivings for mastery of the unconscious and to the possibilities of gratification which are
open to the primitive impulses.   And now it became an ir-
resistibly tempting task, indeed, a scientific duty, to extend
the psycho-analytical methods of investigation from their
original field to more distant and diverse spheres of mental
interest.   The psycho-analytical treatment of patients also
pointed insistently in this direction, since it became evident
that individual forms of the neuroses showed a marked correspondence with the most highly valued products of our civ-
ilisation.   The hysteric is undoubtedly a poet, though he represents his phantasies essentially by mimicry, without considering whether other people understand them or not.   The
ceremonials and prohibitions of obsessional patients force us
to conclude that they have created a private religion for themselves; and even the delusions of the paranoiac show an un-
welcome external similarity and inner relationship to the systems of our philosophers.   We cannot get away from the impression that patients are making, in an asocial manner, the
same attempts at a solution of their conflicts and an appeasement of their urgent desires which, when carried out in a
manner acceptable to a large number of persons, are called
poetry, religion and philosophy.

In an extremely brilliant and suggestive monograph
[Die Bedeutung der Psychoanalyse für die Geisteswissen-
schaften, 1913], O. Rank and H. Sachs have collected the results which have so far been accomplished by the application
of psycho-analysis to the fields of mental interest.   Mythology
and the history of literature and religion appear to furnish
the most easily accessible material.   The final formula which
shall assign to the myth its particular province has not yet

been found.   But in a large work on the incest complex, O.
Rank [Das Inzestmotiv in Dichtung und Sage, Leipzig, 1912]
reaches the remarkable conclusion that the selection of subject matter, particularly in dramatic poetry, is limited chiefly by the range of the Oedipus complex, as it is called in
psycho-analysis.   Through the elaboration of this complex into the most manifold variants, distortions and disguises, the
poet seeks to elucidate his most personal attitude to this effective theme.   It is in the mastery of his Oedipus complex,
i. e. his affective attitude towards his family, and in its nar-
rower sense his father and mother, that the individual comes
to grief, and therefore it is this complex which regularly
forms the kernel of his neurosis.   It owes its significance
not to any unintelligible concatenation of events.   The importance of the parental relationship springs naturally from
the biological fact of the long helplessness and slow maturing
of the young human being, and the complicated development
of his capacity for love; and furthermore guarantees that the
lines on which the Oedipus complex is overcome shall run
parallel with those on which the archaic and animal inheritance
of mankind is most successfully brought under subjection.
In this inheritance are contained all the energies necessary
for the later cultural development of the individual, but they
have first to be sorted out and elaborated.   In the form in
which the individual brings it with him into the world it is
useless for the purposes of social life.

One step more is necessary before we reach the
starting point for a psycho-analytical consideration of religious life.   What is now the heritage of the individual was
once, long ago, a newly acquired possession, handed on from
one generation to another.   The Oedipus complex itself must
therefore have its own process of development, and the study
of prehistory can help us to find out something about it.
Such a study leads us to assume that the human family as
we know it to-day was organised differently in remote primitive times, and this surmise is supported by data obtained
from primitive races of the present day.   If we submit the
prehistoric and ethnological material relating to this archaic
heritage to psycho-analytical elaboration, we come to an un-
expectedly definite conclusion--namely, that god the father at
one time walked incarnate on the earth and exercised his
sovereignty as leader of the hordes of primitive men until
his sons combined together and slew him; and further, that
the first social ties, the basic moral restrictions, and the

oldest form of religion--totemism--originated as a result of, and a reaction against, this liberating misdeed. Later religions are filled with the same content and with the endeavour to obliterate the traces of that crime, or to expiate it by substituting other solutions for the conflict between father and sons; while, on the other hand, they cannot refrain from repeating anew the removal of the father. As a result we can recognise in myths the echo of that occurrence which throws its gigantic shadow over the whole development of mankind.

This hypothesis, founded on the views of Robertson Smith, and developed by me in my Totem und Tabu in 1912, has been taken by Th. Reik as the basis for his studies on the problems of the psychology of religion, of which this is the first volume. In accordance with psycho-analytical technique he begins by considering details of religious life that have not been previously understood, and in elucidating them throws light upon the fundamental presuppositions and ultimate aims of religion. He keeps steadily in view the relationship between prehistoric man and primitive man of to-day, as well as the connection between cultural activities and neurotic substitutive formations. For the rest, the reader may be referred to the author's own introduction. It is to be hoped that his work will commend itself to the attention of those who are most competent to appreciate it.

In the winter of 1961 a "Midwestern apostle of
unreconstructed liberalism" set out, reluctantly at
first but with growing eloquence and purpose, to
serve under President Kennedy as Permanent Representative (Ambassador) to the United Nations.
Looking Outward, his first collection of speeches
and articles appearing two and a half years later,
is an eloquent and persuasive exposition of the role
of the United States in helping to maintain peace in
the world. One immediate service it rendered was
to make crystal clear that violence is not the way
to settle international arguments, that violence can
lead only to incalculable consequences.

Few would think of Adlai Stevenson as an angry
man. He was universally admired for his wit, his
sensitivity, his eloquence, his kindness, and his
ability to talk with notable clarity about things which
politicians inevitably make ambiguous and abstruse.
But in Looking Outward there is one sharp flash of
anger when he crossed swords in a bitter exchange
with Ambassador Zorin of the Soviet Union at the
time of the Cuban missile crisis. When Zorin
charged that the enlarged photographs, which were
displayed at the Security Council meeting to show
the existence of missile sites, were falsified evidence, Stevenson retorted by demanding a simple
"yes" or "no" answer as to whether the Soviets had
installed missiles there. This dialogue then took
place:

Z. I do not wish to answer a question that is
put to me in the fashion in which a prosecutor
puts questions. In due course, Sir, you will
have your answer.

S. You are in the courtroom of world opinion. You have denied they exist, and I want to know if I understood you correctly. I am prepared to wait for my answer until hell freezes over, if that is your decision.

Stevenson's basic conviction as presented in Looking Outward, skillfully buttressed by argument and example, was that the sole purpose of our membership in the United Nations was to find calm and peaceful solutions to the problems which faced the Security Council and General Assembly. His problem here was twofold: first, to convince the skeptical Soviets that his persuasive words represented the opinion of a majority of the people of the United States, and second, perhaps no less difficult, to insure a solid backing among his own people for certain positions which were antithetical to the existing cold war attitude of many Americans at this time. His accomplishment is reflected in these addressed by his pivotal role in standing off Soviet interference in the developing crisis in the Congo in 1961 ("the goal of the United Nations is to establish conditions under which the Congolese people themselves can peacefully work out their own future"), his advocacy of a test ban treaty ("there is only one safe and sure way to stop nuclear tests, and to stop them quickly: that is to conclude a treaty prohibiting all nuclear weapons tests under effective controls"), and his successful advocacy of joint cooperation in space exploration ("In our judgment, the wrong way is to allow the march of science to become a runaway race into the unknown. The right way is to make it an ordered, peaceful, cooperative search under the aegis of the United Nations"). In a short but thoughtful introduction to Looking Outward, John F. Kennedy flatly states his support of Stevenson at a time when senior staff members at the White House were subtly downgrading him. He went on to applaud Stevenson for his diplomacy at the practical and moral level which "has played no small part in helping to confine the crises to the council chambers where they belong."

When Adlai Stevenson accepted President Kennedy's offer to appoint him to the United Nations post, he is reputed to have said that he wanted a

voice in making decisions: "I don't want to be a
lawyer arguing a case whether he believes it or not;
I'm not just interested in explaining or defending a
policy." Whether or not he succeeded in nailing
down this requirement at the time of his appoint-
ment, there can be no doubt that he was widely con-
sulted on foreign policy issues even though some of
the major decisions by-passed the United Nations or
consultation came after the fact. At times this
caused him severe embarrassment but because of a
profound sense of duty to his country and of obligation to Presidents, he continued to give the best he
had. After President Johnson's inauguration he per-
ceived a hardening of attitudes and a failure to anti-
cipate the consequences of certain decisions by the
State Department and the White House. It became increasingly difficult for him to maintain the facade of
unanimity. His dilemma was illustrated chillingly by
a caricature in a French weekly at the time of his
death by heart attack on a sidewalk in London. The
caricature pictured Stevenson falling backwards, his
knees bending, his hands clasped in supplication over
his heart, and his eyes staring upward in horror at
the public menace of two falling bombs overhead--
Vietnam and Santo Domingo.

In his years at the United Nations, in addition to
attending sessions of the Security Council and the
General Assembly, as well as hundreds of commit-
tee meetings, Stevenson managed to accept numerous
speaking engagements each week. Several of these
talks are included in Looking Outward--a tribute to
Robert Frost, a commencement address at Radcliffe,
a defense of the institution of Father's Day, and a
eulogy to Eleanor Roosevelt. At the memorial service for Mrs. Roosevelt, Stevenson paid her the
finest compliment any human being can make to another: "I have never known her equal for objectivity,
for unbiased judgment, for a sort of divine fairness
and simplicity which sprang from the fact that she
never felt her own interests or status or reputation
to be involved in her activities." In all of these
talks, as distinguished from his official speeches at
the United Nations, the reader savors once again the
flashing phrase, the wit, the penetrating and sinewy
mind, and the magnanimity of soul which character-

ized so largely his talk and activity during the presidential campaigns of 1952 and 1956.

PREFACE BY JOHN F. KENNEDY

to Adlai Stevenson's
Looking Outward: Years of Crisis
at the United Nations

This collection of speeches and papers offers a valuable tour d'horizon of contemporary American foreign policy in all of its scope and variety. In particular, this work will give its readers a fresh and full understanding of the reasons why the United States supports the United Nations and why that institution so well serves our national interest.

Many crises have threatened the peace of the world since Adlai Stevenson became the United States Ambassador to the United Nations. The force, eloquence and courage with which he has advanced the American viewpoint have played no small part in helping to confine those crises to the council chambers where they belong. Looking Outward is, in consequence, no academic or textbook exposition of our foreign policy in the United Nations. It is rather a running discourse on some of the most electric events of our time. It is thought generated on the spot, not hindsight called up in tranquility; it is the voice of Ambassador Stevenson, quickened by crisis. That, of course, is the heart of the UN's existence--to provide a forum in which the clash of ideas in healthy debate will supplant the clash of arms in deadly combat. That it may do so with steadily mounting success is our hope in this age when man's capacity to wreak destruction still overshadows his ability to reach the stars.

Our belief in the indispensability of the United Nations does not, of course, mean that we are in total agreement with every decision the United Nations might take. What it does mean is that we are a nation of laws--and that we respect the law of nations. So it follows that we invest the highest hope in the organization which encourages all nations, large and small, to walk the same path of justice and progress we ourselves have chosen in our own history. In sup-

JOHN F. KENNEDY

porting the United Nations, we not only support aims and ideals inscribed in our own Constitution, but we work to convert the high goals of our own foreign policy into living reality: the achievement of a world community of independent states living together in free association, in liberty and in peace.

I was present as a member of the press when the United Nations was organized in San Francisco in 1945. Governor Stevenson was there too for the Department of State, although he wasn't making as many speeches as he does now. Nor was I--but we have both made up for our silence in the years since.

During his presidential campaigns Governor Stevenson raised the level of our national political dialogue. As our representative in the United Nations, he has similarly raised the level of the international political dialogue. The proof lies in the pages which follow.

John F. Kennedy

JAMES D. McCALLUM

"He began as a painter," wrote J. B. Priestley in the London Mercury for May, 1926, "and still brings to literature a painter's eye, delighted in the colors and shapes and textures, the more luxurious the better." Certainly Java Head (1918), the fifth novel by Philadelphia-born Joseph Hergesheimer, is a journey of sheer enchantment into the bright world of color. Take for example the clear sunlit view of the square-rigger Nautilis approaching the harbor: "The ship moved more slowly, under her topsails and jibs, in a soundless progress with the ripples falling away in water like dark green glass, liquid and still." Or take one of the numerous descriptions of Taou Yuen's dress. She wore "a long gown with wide sleeves of blue-black satin, embroidered in peach-colored flower petals and innumerable minute sapphire and orange butterflies, a short sleeveless jacket of sage green caught with looped red jade buttons and threaded with silver and indigo, and high-soled slippers crusted and tasselled with pearls." What we have here is a sensitive and sensuous impression that almost seems to be painted in colors instead of words.

The story of Java Head, which is the name of the family home and symbolizes "the safe and happy end of an arduous voyage," concerns the shipowning family of Ammidon in Old Salem around the middle of the nineteenth century. Jeremy Ammidon, founder of the family's fortunes, now retired, is an irascible though loveable old autocrat who thinks "it is only reasonable that a country's got to be run like a ship, from the quarter deck." But Salem's mast-crowded harbor activity, the world Jeremy knew and

loved so well, is about over. William, the oldest
son, now largely responsible for running the business, contrives to replace the blunt-nosed square
riggers with the newer, fast clipper ships and to
secure a part of the prosperous California gold-
rush trade. All this has to be done surreptitiously
because of his father's violent opposition to change.
One day the youngest son, Gerrit, having been given
up for lost at sea, sails into harbor with a cargo
rich in spoils and a new wife, Taou Yuen, a Chinese woman of the highest caste "as exotic as a
perfumed Oriental vase." Exposed to the gossip
and deviousness of Salem's society, Taou Yuen re-
mains imperturbable and alien. She treats con-
temptuously the advances of Edward Dunsack, the
one person in Salem who is familiar with the Chinese language and culture, but who has become de-
moralized by smoking opium. Through him she
learns to suspect her husband's fidelity, and, in
the end, dreading Dunsack's touch and knowing that
she can never be happy in Salem, kills herself.

Java Head is no ordinary novel. In his introduction to a new edition of the novel, James D.
McCallum, teacher and humanist and at one time
professor of English at Dartmouth College, writes
"The insistence on life itself, rather than on the
thesis of life, takes Hergesheimer out of the class
of moralizing novelists." We imagine the past as
more disciplined and serene than the present. It
is not so. When we look into the lives and times
of the characters in Java Head, we find them just
as turbulent and erratic as our own. McCallum's
epitaph for the novel: "First life itself, characters
diverse and influencing one another; then the background, clearly and accurately depicted; and from
this combination described with what we call truth,
comes the idea of the novel."

PRAISE FROM FAMOUS MEN

INTRODUCTION BY JAMES D. McCALLUM

to Joseph Hergesheimer's
Java Head

The scene of Java Head is Salem, a town of the past,
with a past, a sort of Sargossa Sea in which lie the hulks
alike of the full-bottomed vessels, beloved of Jeremy Ammidon, and of the more swiftly sailing clippers to which he
was ever opposed--all Ichabods of the China trade.   Whatever glory they had--and they were glorious, romantic, and
picturesque--is now to be recovered only in tales about
them, and from the point of view of the present generation
they are phantom ships.   So it is a temptation to a novelist
to lay his scene in Salem, and, by a sort of novelised anti-
quarianism, to call up again the voices of silent sea-faring
men, full rig those phantom ships, and let them beat their
way to other picturesque and Oriental ports for romantic
cargoes of tea and spices and boxes of contraband opium.
The Sargossa Sea is white for a while then with unfurled
sails and sails unfurling--"and the midshipmen running
about"--and when the story closes, the wind dies away and
the voices, and the antiquarian is finished.

But Salem means much more than that to Hergesheimer.   It is a port of dramatic conflict, of the struggle between the old shipping and the new; of "astrolabe and the
moon" against "chronometers with confounded rates of vari-
ation and other fancy parlor instruments to read your position from"; of responsibility for the cargo divided among the
crew as against "closed capital"; of bold trading, hazardous
and somewhat haphazard, against "Boston store" methods of
business, not bold, not so hazardous, and anything but haphazard; the methods of Grandfather Ammidon, himself almost
a hulk, against those of his cautious son William, a lands-
man; the romance of shipping against the commercialism of
trading.   In a word, between old and new business methods.

Such is the conflict to which Hergesheimer introduces
the reader at the beginning of Java Head.   It is an entrancing
struggle, vividly and briefly told, and, as we read, we side
unconsciously with the old captain, even though he does argue
himself to an ominous purple, and even though his methods
are inefficient.   He has the fervor of a survivor of lost
causes.

That, however, is only part of the conflict. In Salem
East tries to meet West, and the narrative of that meeting
is proof that never the twain shall meet. Stated in terms of
personalities, Taou Yuen and the inhabitants of Salem can
never sympathise with each other. And this is the tragedy,
less picturesque than the losing battle of Jeremy Ammidon
with his tales of "antediluvian trading voyages," but more
personal, and so more impressive. Into staid Salem, and
in spite of all traditions to the contrary, Gerrit has brought
a Chinese wife, and from the beginning the hopelessness of
Taou Yuen in such an environment is clear. Even from the
moment that he introduces his Manchu lady to the family, the
issue is certain. "Rhoda Ammidon gave an uncontrollable
gasp as the Chinese woman sank in a fluttering prostration
of color at Jeremy's feet. He ejaculated, 'God bless me,'
and started back. William's face was inscrutable, unguessed
lines appeared about his severe mouth. His own sensation
was one of incredulity touched with mounting anger and feeling of outrage." That scene represents in miniature the
brief career of Taou Yuen in Salem. She doesn't fit. No
matter that she too has her high traditions, that her thinking
and living is austere and remote from vulgarity; her ways
are different and cannot be reconciled to Western ways. She
will not, cannot, give over her habits of life, and certainly
Salem will not meet her half way.

That is the personal conflict in Java Head, and the
tragedy is the more poignant because Taou Yuen is such a
slight thing, far removed from a favorable environment,
against so many, secure in their superior Occidentalism and
ignorant of any life but their own.

It is with a marvellous gift of clear expression that
Hergesheimer pictures the isolation of Taou Yuen in the
midst of those whose bread and butter and finery and wealth
have come from trading with and on her own people. One
would not expect the town to accept her, but would not the
members of the family, ultimately? By no means. Sidsall,
for instance, goes up to Taou Yuen's room after breakfast,
watches her make her elaborate toilet, and is fascinated.
"It's very beautiful," she exclaims. But then Taou Yuen
touches her. "The cold sharp contact of the long curving
finger guard gave the girl an unpleasant shock. It seemed
lifeless, or like the scratching of a beetle. Suddenly the
woman's glittering gaze, her expressionless face stiff with

paint, the blaze of her barbaric colors, filled Sidsall with a shrinking that was almost dread." That sums up the feeling toward Taou Yuen. She is in the house, to be sure; as the wife of Gerrit she has to be; but she never becomes a member of the household, acceptable emotionally. And when Gerrit prepares to take her to church, Salem revolts again, and would keep her apart, an isolated, curious specimen. "That's unheard of," William exclaimed heatedly; "a woman in all her paint and perfume and outrageous clothes in North Church, with--my family! I won't have it, do you understand." "No worse than what you see there every week," Gerrit retorted calmly; "corsets and feathers and female gimcracks. Plenty of rouge and cologne too. It will give them something new to stare at and whisper about." So too the Salem ladies repulse her with their curiosity and ignorance: "A Chinese wedding must be very gay, with firecrackers and--." Taou Yuen explains to them how dignified the wedding is, but she does not convince them. "I'm told polygamy is an active practice," Mrs. Wibird remarks with a rising interest. And Mrs. Wibird and the rest are not interested in the denial that follows. Gerrit had brought back a splendid cargo, and even if he was seven months overdue, he had added profits to the company; but he should have known better than add this item to his cargo.

So Taou Yuen stands alone, trying to avoid the more brutally curious of Salem and to maintain the high-minded virtues to which she had been bred. One alone in Salem-- at least of those who appear in the novel--has any intimacy with Chinese ways: Edward Dunsack, the opium addict, a coarse, jealous, fibreless derelict, to whom China has meant nothing but lust. Some of the externals of Taou Yuen's native environment he does know, but at the beauty of it he sneers and considers her simply as a woman of the streets. One other item Gerrit might well have omitted from his cargo: the box of opium which he brought to Edward. On the one ship came the victim and the means of her death. Edward destroys himself with the opium; but the means of his destruction is the very poison which is Taou Yuen's salvation from contamination with him. As he tries to touch her--he has cornered her in Nettie Vollar's room--she sweeps up the opium balls, swallows the poison, and so saves herself.

This is the tragedy of <u>Java Head</u>, and anyone who

reads may see it for himself. And now a question, gentle
reader. Are we not something like those members of the
Ammidon family and the other inhabitants of Salem! Does
not the suicide of Taou Yuen furnish almost a happy ending
for you and me? Here is Gerrit, a man who in a burst of
sympathy clearly made a mistake by marrying a Chinese
woman. We share something of the feeling of Salem toward
him. How could he do such a thing? What can he ever hope
to do tied down to such a mate? Has he not lost by this
marriage the profound emotional experience which Salem--
and you and I--would wish for him? Is there no way out?

And the suicide solves the problem, and sets Gerrit
free to marry the woman who had attracted him before he set
out for China on the trip that resulted in his unwise marriage.
We forget that Nettie Vollar is an outcast in Salem; we forget too that she cannot pretend to the dignity and high-minded-
ness of Taou Yuen. All her shortcomings we overlook--be-
cause she is a white woman, and so much more suitable to
Gerrit. Thus the ending is <u>almost</u> happy. Gerrit is free of
his Chinese wife; he must be happy now married to a white
woman, even with a bar sinister. At least he has satisfied
one of the conventions.

Gerrit had a "quick heart and an honest disdain for
the muddling narrow way of the land. " His impetuosity made
him the daring captain that he was, ashamed to take in sail
even at the risk of losing a spar; it made him too the husband of Taou Yuen. He did what he wanted to do. And his
interest in Nettie Vollar was in the nature of a protest, so
Jeremy Ammidon thought, against the smugness of Salem
opinion. He typifies in <u>Java Head</u> the revolt against com-
placency and conformity.

Gerrit belongs to a group of characters favored by
Hergesheimer. He is an example of Hergesheimer's forceful
man, the man of strong will or of strong passion who drives
through to his goal, overcoming the opposition of individual
rivals or of society. Such figures are of course found throughout literature; Hergesheimer has simply recognised the possibilities of this character for artistic treatment, and has drawn
him often enough to demand recognition from any critic of his
work. Alexander Hulings in <u>Tubal Cain</u> is a good example.
Hulings, when the story opens, is a poor lawyer, a man of
ability, but he has not found himself. He suddenly resolves

to abandon his profession, and enters the iron industry. Beginning humbly and forced to overcome almost disastrous competition, he succeeds by dint of much physical exertion and his strong will in conquering his rivals, ultimately marries the daughter of his greatest rival, and becomes iron master of a wide territory.

A critic has seen in this striving of Hergesheimer's heroes a reflection of the novelist's own striving for public recognition. The comparison is interesting and plausible.

Then the men who defy society. Howat Penny, son of a leading family, courts, if courting it is, a woman socially much his inferior, just as Gerrit does. So much has the theme appealed to Hergesheimer that he has based The Three Black Pennys on the recurrence of this "blackness" in representatives of the Penny family throughout the last century. And the hero of Balisand does as he wishes, opposing his own likings to those of his companions. It is clear accordingly that Gerrit is not an isolated example. The strength of these révoltés, their reality, is to a great extent the measure of Hergesheimer's power.

Contrasted with such a strong-willed character, Roger Brevard is colorless, because Roger accepts the conventions of Salem. He is decorous, careful, plodding, and totally lacking in the spirit of adventure; and the part he plays in the novel, seemingly an unimportant part, has significance in throwing into relief the scornful and reckless Gerrit. Only once does Roger assert himself. He has heard that Sidsall, with whom he is in love, is to go abroad for study, and he resolves to act. After supper he goes home, brooding over his information, and as a protest to his orderly habits, and as a gesture of defiance to the conventions--he leaves his clothes in a disorderly heap! His passion was carrying him away. "Then, unable to dismiss the thought of how crumpled his trousers would be in the morning, oppressed by the picture of the tumbled garments, he finally rose and, in the dark, relaid them in the familiar smooth array." In the morning he braves William and Rhoda, the parents of Sidsall, declares his love for her, and she declares her love for him. But they want a man "nearer Sidsall's age." "Roger Brevard winced. He tried to say something about hope and the future--. He turned away, crushed by convention, filled with shame and a sense of self-betrayal." Then to the harbor,

where the respectable, conventional Roger sees the ship of
the adventuring ones, Gerrit and his wife, who had asked
permission of no one, sail away from him. "The color and
the vividness of his existence had been withdrawn."

*   *   *   *

Java Head is bright with the color of life--of setting,
of diverse characters, of human passions. The tradition runs
that Hergesheimer studied ninety-five volumes on the subject
matter of the novel as part preparation for his writing; and
although it would be unwise to stress this study--the reader
might be led to expect an historical novel--it is certainly
worthwhile to observe that by means of it Hergesheimer has
been able to picture not only the larger externals, the town
and the ships and the cargoes, but the smaller details as
well, the minutiae of dress, for example. Hergesheimer is
master of the concrete word. His use of sea-terms is accurate; his technical vocabulary quite remarkable. Take this
example of his description: "It was an accepted fact now that
Taou Yuen, the Garden of Peaches, stayed in her room until
long after breakfast; and when Sidsall, rising from the table,
found a servant taking up a pot of hot water for tea, she se-
cured it and knocked carefully on the door above. The slur-
ring hesitating voice said 'Come in,' and she entered with a
diffidence covered by a cheerfully polite morning greeting.
She found the other in crêpe de Chine pantaloons tightly
wrapped about her ankles and bound over quilted muslin socks
with gay brocaded ribbons and a short floating gown of gray
silk worked with willow leaves. Her hair was an undisturbed
complication of lustrous black, gold bodkins, and flowers
massed on either side; and her face, without paint or powder,
was as smooth as ivory and the color of very pale coffee and
cream." It is because Hergesheimer knows his subject that
he describes convincingly; he avoids the lazy general word.
He becomes, in other words, a connoisseur of the particular
period or situation or subject matter.

Such an exhibition of things, however, would be no
more than a museum display were it not for the diversified
and individualised characters and elements of the novel. The
primness and self-consciousness of the eleven-year old
Laurel; the irascibility and deep-water frankness of old Jeremy; the floor-walker manner of William; the misanthropy of
Barzil; the grossness of Edward; the grace and wistfulness

101

of Taou Yuen; the grayness and meekness of Nettie; pride in
whole-hearted adventure, parental watchfulness, sexual lust,
submission to convention and the flouting of it, starved lives
and lives developed--these, to mention no more, bring to life
the setting.   And all within such a small compass, because
Java Head is a comparatively short novel.   With an economy
that is rewarded with clearness of effect, Hergesheimer has
devoted a chapter to a character, drawn each character to
life, and so built up his story.

* * * *

This insistence on life itself, rather than on the thesis
of life, takes Hergesheimer out of the class of moralizing
novelists.   Although there is a definite core of thought--I
have tried to make clear what that core is--the novel is not
primarily a protest against small town life or narrow nationalism or the "ungirt loin and the unlit lamp."   First life
itself, characters diverse and influencing one another; then
the background, clearly and accurately depicted; and from
this combination described with what we call truth, comes
the idea of the novel.   Of course Hergesheimer must direct
the reader; any novelist must; but he directs with the wise
restraint of the writer who knows that the function of the
novelist is to make his characters live and that it is the duty
of the preacher or pamphliteer to erect signboards of conduct.

* * * *

The story of Hergesheimer's life can be quickly told
so far as the external facts of dates and localities are concerned.   He was born in Philadelphia, February 15, 1880.
Interesting for the study of his novels is the fact that some
of his ancestors--he comes of Pennsylvania Dutch stock--
made their money in the iron foundries.   As a boy, Hergesheimer writes, he was averse to study.   For a while he attended a Quaker school, and at the age of seventeen, the
Academy of Fine Arts in Philadelphia.   At the Academy he
does not seem to have accomplished much, "doing one day's
work in fifteen."   Then came a legacy from a "Presbyterian
foundryman," and with it Hergesheimer traveled to Venice,
and soon spent it all.   He records: "I had a private gondola
with a Turkey-red carpet and my initials in silver on the
gondolier's sleeve."   Whether or not that was his main ex-

travagance he has not noted; at any rate he enjoyed himself, went through his legacy, and returned to the United States with a remainder of twenty-five cents.   Then followed a period of rather tentative living, or if you like, of jolly night life in Philadelphia (see his "Some Veracious Paragraphs" in the Bookman, 1918), his "walking trip" to Harper's Ferry--it was on this trip that Hergesheimer was inspired to try his hand at novel writing--and his marriage in 1907.   Following is a list of his more important writings: The Lay Anthony, 1914; Mountain Blood, 1915; The Three Black Pennys, 1917; Gold and Iron, 1918; Java Head, 1919; The Happy End, 1919; Linda Condon, 1919; Hugh Walpole, 1919; Cytherea, 1922; Tubal Cain, 1922; The Dark Fleece, 1922; The Bright Shawl, 1922; Balisand, 1924.

JAMES DOW McCALLUM

ARCHIBALD MacLEISH

In his 1967 address on the occasion of the Carl
Sandburg Memorial Ceremony, the distinguished
American poet Archibald MacLeish stated that Sandburg's principal achievement was his credulity and
belief in man: "those who are credulous about the
destiny of man, who believe more than they can
prove of the future of the human race, will make
that future, shape that destiny." To those who came
to manhood during the period when the bomb was
dropped, the White House bugged, and J. Edgar
Hoover knew everything about everybody, such cred-
ulousness may seen unrealistic, even effete. In
Sandburg's case, it is not. His life and work represent a bulwark against delusion, lying, and decep-
tion. Sandburg was a genuine democrat; democratic
ideas seemed part of his flesh and blood. His sense
of equality and belief in man was a direct product of
his democratic ideas. Without nationalistic ballyhoo
or mawkish sentiment, he expressed these ideas in
verse which portrayed the spirit, strength, and revo-
lutionary gusto of the American people.

Sandburg was born the son of a Swedish black-
smith who emigrated to this country and found work
on the Illinois railroad. Carl grew up in Galesburg,
Illinois, attended school there but dropped out at the
age of thirteen (like his progenitor, Walt Whitman),
and from then until he was seventeen took on a variety of unskilled jobs including driving a milk wagon,
working in a brick factory, and making balls in a
pottery. He then went west to work in the wheat
fields and in railroad construction, only to return
home in a couple of years to become an apprentice
to a house painter. For a short period he served

in the Spanish-American War and after his discharge entered Lombard (now Knox) College where he became editor of the college newspaper. Some very special elixir evidently got into his veins at Lombard because by the time he graduated he had developed a lifelong interest in journalism and poetry.

Neither the forbidding size of Sandburg's published poems, nearly 700 pages spanning a generation of verse in the Harcourt Brace edition of The Complete Poems, nor his own solemn foreword to this edition should put one off. His poetry is easy to read, stimulating, spirited, almost conversational. Neither brilliant nor profound, he is wise and humane, insatiably curious about all facets of American life and people--Lincoln, Washington, day laborers, millionaires, Negroes, Greeks, prize-fighters, mothers suckling their young, Jews selling fish, cities, farms, and the masses who lived and worked there. If one doubts that a poet can entertain while instructing, begin with "Cool Tombs," "Wilderness," "Bargoyle," "Soup," and "A Fence."

ARCHIBALD MacLEISH
"A Memorial Tribute
to Carl Sandburg"

Back in the nineteen thirties Carl Sandburg published some lines in which he recorded the convictions of a Chicago poet.

One of the early Chicago poets,
One of the slouching underslung Chicago poets,
Having only the savvy God gave him,
Lacking a gat, lacking brass knucks,
Having one lead pencil to spare, wrote:

'I am credulous about the destiny of man,
and I believe more than I can ever prove
of the future of the human race
and the importance of illusions....'

105

No one who knew Sandburg would identify this as a self-portrait. Sandburg, though he sometimes slouched, was never underslung. There are, however, likenesses: traits and associations in common. There was Chicago--even, one might say from here, early Chicago. There was that one lead pencil to spare. And there was, more obviously, the talk. Some will hear Sandburg's living voice, as I do, in "the importance of illusions." But the principal likeness, of course, is in the credo itself. Sandburg too was credulous about the destiny of man and believed more than he could ever prove of the future of the human race. Indeed it was precisely because he so believed and was thus credulous that he became the poet whose death has brought us here this afternoon--here not only to Washington but to this particular place in Washington. For this particular place is also committed to an unprovable and as yet unproved belief in the future of the human race; a credulity about the destiny of man.

Poets are not comparable. They are not, as the lawyers used to say, fungible, interchangeable like grains of wheat. You cannot measure one against another saying this one is larger or more durable than that one--"greater" as the text-books put it. What foot-rule will measure the comparative dimensions of Walt Whitman and Emily Dickinson, of Sappho and Sophocles, of Dante and Donne? Poets, when they are poets, are as unique as poems are when they are actually poems: which is to say incomparably unique, essentially themselves.

But although poets can't be compared they can be distinguished. And one of the most elementary distinctions is that between the poet, however "great," whose achievement is in a particular poem or poems, and the poet, however incomparable, whose achievement is in the work as a whole, the body of the work, all sorts and kinds and degrees bound up together. Frost spoke unforgettably for the first when he said at a dinner in Amherst on his eightieth birthday that he hoped to leave behind "a few poems that will be hard to get rid of"--which, of course, he did--and more than a few--and far more than "hard to get rid of" ... though perhaps nothing is really "more" than that. Sandburg might stand, in our own time at least, for the second. With Sandburg it is the body of the work that weighs, the sum of it, a whole quite literally greater than the total of its parts.

And what creates that whole, what binds the parts together, is, of course, precisely the credulity confessed by
that slouching underslung Chicago poet.   Sandburg had a sub-
ject--and the subject was belief in man.   You find it everywhere.   You find it announced in the title of the book in
which his Chicago poet appears: The People, Yes.   You find
it in one form or another throughout the hundred odd poems
and proses of which that extraordinary book is composed.
You find it in other poems.   And in other books.   Most important of all, you find it in the echo which all these poems
and these books leave in the ear--your ear and the ears of
others: the echo which has made the body of Sandburg's work
a touchstone for two generations of readers--almost, by this
time, for three.

A touchstone of what?   A touchstone of America.   If
ever a man wrote for a particular people, however he may
have reached in his heart for all people, it was Sandburg.

Between Amarilla and the North Pole
is only a barb wire fence...

Out here the only windbreak
is the North Star.

And if ever a man was heard by those he wrote for it was
Carl.   Europeans, even the nearest in that direction, the
English, do not truly understand him but Americans do.
There is a raciness in the writing, in the old, strict sense
of the word raciness: a tang, a liveliness, a pungency,
which is native and natural to the American ear.   And under-
neath the raciness, like the smell of earth under the vividness
of rain, there is a seriousness which is native too--the kind
of human, even mortal, seriousness you hear in Lincoln.

An American touchstone.   But is there not a contra-
diction here?   Can a body of work bound together by credulity
constitute a touchstone for Americans?   For Americans now?
Once, perhaps, in the generation of Jefferson, or once again
in the generation of Lincoln--but now?   There is a notion
around in great parts of the world--in Asia and in certain
countries of Europe--that America has changed in recent
years: that the last thing one can expect from America or
from Americans today is credulity.   It is asserted that the
American people have now, as the saying goes, grown up.
That they have put aside childish things, beliefs which can't

be proved. That they have come to see what the world is,
to put their trust in the certainties of power. That they have
become, in brief, what is favorably known as "realistic":
about themselves, about humanity, about the destiny of man.

Listening to contemporary speeches, reading the papers, one can see where these opinions of America may have
come from. But are they true? Are they really true? Can
we believe, in this place, thinking of this man, that they are
true? Sandburg was an American. He was an American also of our time, of our generation. He died fifty-seven days
ago. He was seen and known and talked to by many in this
meeting. His struggles were the struggles of the generation
to which most of us belong--the struggles of the great depression and the many wars and the gathering racial crisis
and all the rest. He was a man of our time who lived in
our time, laughed at the jokes our time has laughed at, shed
its tears. And yet Sandburg was a credulous man--a man
credulous about humanity--a man who believed more than he
could prove about humanity. And Sandburg, though he listened to those who thought themselves realists, though he
was attentive to the hard-headed, was not convinced by them.
In The People, Yes it is said:

> "The strong win against the weak.
> The strong lose against the stronger.
> And across the bitter years and the howling winters
> the deathless dream will be the stronger ...
>
> Shall man always go on dog-eat-dog?
> Who says so?
> The stronger?
> And who is the stronger?..."

What Sandburg knew and said was what America knew from
the beginning and said from the beginning and has not yet, no
matter what is believed of her, forgotten how to say: that
those who are credulous about the destiny of man, who believe more than they can prove of the future of the human
race, will make that future, shape that destiny. This was
his great achievement: that he found a new way in an in-
credulous and disbelieving and often cynical time to say what
Americans have always known. And beyond that there was
another and even greater achievement: that the people listened. They are listening still.

PAUL C. MANGELSDORF

"Mein Zeit will schon kommen" (My time will come one of these days), the nineteenth-century Austrian monk, Gregor Mendel, is reported to have said, but unfortunately the brilliant amateur who is today looked upon as the father of the science of genetics died without attracting the attention of the learned world. He was too far ahead of his time. His discovery in a small monastery garden of a new law of nature--a predictable pattern of inheritance-- was not brought to light until sixteen years after his death and thirty-four years after the publication of his experiments with edible peas.

It is doubtful in these days whether anyone but the dusting maid in a university library has touched the volume of the proceedings of the Brünn Natural History Society in which Father Mendel's treatise first appeared. Entitled Experiments in Plant Hybridisation, it was published in the original German text in 1866 following its presentation in two lectures before the forty learned members of the Brünn Society the year before. Exchange copies were distributed to research libraries in Europe and the United States but nobody read the work and it seemed bound for oblivion. Then a German botanist named W. O. Focke listed it in his bibliography in 1881. By the end of the century three scientists, working independently on the problem which Mendel had studied, discovered his work through the bibliography. Before 1900 was out he was hailed throughout Europe as one of the world's great discoverers. His treatise became a standard reference work and was translated into English many times after 1900.

When the writings of a great man are discovered

and reprinted frequently, it is customary to insert a
preface in front of them. The story of Father Gregor
Mendel's memorable scientific achievement is made
all the more impressive in the factual, calm prose
of Dr. Paul C. Mangelsdorf's foreword to the Harvard University Press centennial reprint of Experiments in Plant Hybridisation (1965). The facts as
presented by Mangelsdorf, formerly Fisher Professor of Natural History at Harvard, are overwhelm-
ing--(1) "first experiments on inheritance that were
based on carefully chosen contrasting traits," (2)
"first experiments that classified the forms that appeared following hybridization not only in the first
and second generation but also in succeeding generations," (3) "the first botanical experiments in
which a successful attempt was made to ascertain
statistical relations between the forms," and (4) the
"first experiments in which a problem in biology had
been sharply defined, reduced to its essentials, and
attacked with a carefully designed experiment." In
the light of all this it is not surprising that Kevin
Guinagh should describe Gregor Mendel's experience
in his book Inspired Amateurs as yet "another instance of an inspired, but in his day unappreciated,
amateur pointing out a higher ground to the profes-
sionals."

FOREWORD BY PAUL C. MANGELSDORF

to Gregor Mendel's
Experiments in Plant Hybridisation

The year 1965 marks the centennial of one of the
great scientific events of all time. In February and March
1865, the Austrian monk, Gregor Mendel, a modest scholar
of peasant origin and ancestry, gave two lectures to the
Natural History Society of Brünn of which he was one of the
founders. The lectures were concerned with experiments on
hybridization of garden peas which he had conducted over a
period of eight years in a small monastery garden about 15
ft wide and 30 to 40 ft long. These experiments showed that
the inheritance of characteristics in peas followed definite
statistical rules. Mendel believed that he had discovered

certain valid principles of inheritance.

The lectures attracted little attention at the time; after all Mendel was not a famous scholar but a teacher of physics in the local high school.   They apparently attracted no more attention when his paper of 48 neatly handwritten pages was published the following year in the Proceedings of the Society.   Some historians have supposed that the paper was overlooked because it appeared in an "obscure" journal, but this apparently is not true since the journal had a circulation to about 120 libraries and institutions in Europe and America; in addition Mendel had about 40 reprints at his disposal for private distribution.   The simple fact is that Mendel was ahead of his time.

The author died a disappointed man.   "Mein Zeit will schon kommen" he is reported to have said, but it did not come in his lifetime.   His discoveries were known to Carl von Nägeli, a leader of botanical research and the foremost authority on hybridization, with whom Mendel carried on a considerable correspondence.   But Nägeli was not impressed; indeed he was somewhat patronizing in his replies to Mendel's letters.

Then, in 1900, 16 years after his death, Mendel's principles were dramatically rediscovered within the same year by three botanists: DeVries of Holland, Correns of Germany, and Tschermak of Austria.   By this time, however, in large part because of the profound observations of the German zoologist Weismann, father of the germ plasm theory, the scientific world was ready, and the principles of inheritance had an immediate impact, almost explosive in its nature, upon biological thinking and research.   Correns, himself, suggested in 1901 that Mendel's principles applied to animals as well as to plants.   The proof of this was produced independently in 1902 by Bateson and Cuénot.   In 1903 Farabee showed that albinism in a Negro family was probably a Mendelian recessive characteristic.   Also in 1903 Sutton pointed out that the behavior of the chromosomes has a striking resemblance to the behavior of the hereditary factors postulated by Mendel.   Convincing evidence that the chromosomes are indeed the carriers of heredity came in 1910 with Morgan's report on sex-linked inheritance in the fruit fly, Drosophila.   In 1915, with the publication of "The Mechanism of Mendelian Heredity" by Morgan and his students, Sturtevant, Muller, and Bridges, the chromosome theory of heredity was well established.   Within the next 15 years new insights into the nature and mechanism of evolution had been won; the effects of inbreeding and crossbreeding had been explained in Mendelian terms, and the principles of heredity had been successfully applied to the improvement of cultivated plants and domestic animals.

Today Mendel's experiments are recognized as classic, and we can see that they foreshadowed a powerful new trend in biology.   The experiments were simple; almost anyone could have done them.   But they were the first experiments on inheritance that were based on carefully chosen contrasting traits, for example, round versus wrinkled seeds and yellow versus green seeds.   They were the first experiments that classified the forms that appeared following hybridization not only in the first and second generations but also in succeeding generations, in some cases up to the sixth. These were the first botanical experiments in which a successful attempt was made to ascertain statistical relations between the forms by the simple but novel procedure of counting their numbers.   Indeed they were the first experiments in which a problem in biology had been sharply defined, reduced to its essentials, and attacked with a carefully designed experiment.   It is not surprising that the answers were clear and concise, and the proof decisive.   Mendel's work is a splendid example of what Henry Wallace has called "small gardens and big ideas."   It is also one of the best examples of the preeminence of the human mind as a scientific instrument.

Mendel's experiments showed that heredity is transmitted by particulate elements which follow simple but definite and predictable statistical rules.   These particles, which determine the hereditary traits, occur in pairs in the parents and their offspring and singly in the reproductive cells.   In true breeding parents, such as those employed in Mendel's experiments, the particles of a pair are identical.   In the hybrid offspring the two particles of a pair are unlike but they do not blend or influence each other to produce transitional forms; they are transmitted from generation to generation intact.   The particles are known today as "genes" and their physical basis in all living things from bacteria to man consists of groups of nucleotides on the molecule of DNA, deoxyribonucleic acid.   Thus the universality of the principles of heredity now has its final proof in the universality of the hereditary material.

PAUL C. MANGELSDORF

Harvard University
September 1965

EDNA ST. VINCENT MILLAY

Since personality is more interesting to our age than poetry, it is not surprising to discover that Edna St. Vincent Millay, once regarded as possessing the most individual lyric gift in American verse, is now in partial eclipse. In 1924, after having achieved a considerable measure of success with published verse, she came out with a volume of prose under the nom de plume, Nancy Boyd. It was entitled Distressing Dialogues and it consisted of a collection of small satires, not all of them dialogues, which had appeared previously in Vanity Fair. In this collection the poet, acting as journalist, replicates the absurdities and superficialities of the upper-middle-class milieu in which she lives, but instead of making them a subject of abuse she creates flawlessly comical situations in which to frame them.

It has been suggested that Miss Millay used a pseudonym in publishing Distressing Dialogues because she felt she might be demeaning her lyric talent in the eyes of her reading public. If this were true it did not prevent her from claiming the copyright ownership or providing a characteristically tongue-in-cheek preface in her real name. Miss Millay's high-spirited humor is not constrained within the bounds of her eleven-line preface. What she offers us is a charmingly impudent preliminary flourish to the dozen or more satires which follow and which use laughter and comic situations to expose the pretensions of society.

EDNA ST. VINCENT MILLAY

PREFACE BY EDNA ST. VINCENT MILLAY
to Nancy Boyd's
Distressing Dialogues

Miss Boyd has asked me to write a preface to these dialogues, with which, having followed them eagerly as they appeared from time to time in the pages of Vanity Fair, I was already familiar.   I am no friend of prefaces, but if there must be one to this book, it should come from me, who was its author's earliest admirer.   I take pleasure in recommending to the public these excellent small satires, from the pen of one in whose work I have a never-failing interest and delight.

EDNA ST. VINCENT MILLAY.
Tokyo, May 6, 1924.

Nine Answers by G. Bernard Shaw is a thirty-
six page pamphlet, privately printed for Jerome
Kern in 1923. It has a preface by Christopher Morley. The manuscript was written in 1896 shortly
after Shaw's fortieth birthday.

The text to the pamphlet is divided into two
parts: the first consisting of nine questions concerning the life and work of George Bernard Shaw,
signed with initials C. R. , and the second, com-
prising the responses to the nine questions, signed
G. Bernard Shaw. It may well be a mistake to
divide the contents thusly because Shaw most likely
wrote both parts. The heading of the questions,
Examination Paper /"Corvus: De Vitâ et Operibus
Georgii Bernardi Shaw, " is certainly suggestive of the
hand of a jesting, posturing G.B.S. "Corvus" is the
Latin for "rook"; the initials C. R. , as it turns out,
stand for Clarence Rook, a British author and journalist. The identity of Clarence Rook may not have
been transparent to the fortunate recipients of Jerome
Kern's Christmas present in 1923 (it was not to
Christopher Morley; at least he does not mention
Rook in his preface) but Shaw furnishes the clue to
identification in the final paragraph of his answers.
He is addressing C. R. : "If you have had the patience to wade through all this ... you will have
your materials for a masterly sketch of me. Do as
you like with what I have written ... you need not
fear to be indiscreet by letting it out just as it
stands. Or if you can fake it up otherwise with advantage, so much the better. I can refer other people to the Chap-Book for the next five years when
they come bothering for biographical matter. " And

"fake it up otherwise" is precisely what Clarence
Rook proceeded to do in an article entitled "George
Bernard Shaw, " which appeared in the November 1,
1896, issue of the Chap-Book, published semi-
monthly by Herbert S. Stone & Co. in Chicago.
Rook's version is a highly imaginative across-the-
table interview with Shaw, using all the questions
and answers contained in the pamphlet but so cun-
ningly recast as to make it authentically his own.
Since Herbert S. Stone & Co. published a number
of Shaw's writings in the United States, it is quite
possible that Shaw suggested the Chap-Book as a
suitable place for Rook's reconstruction of the nine
answers. At any rate, Shaw was well pleased with
Rook's article. Midway in Dan Laurence's edition
of Shaw's Collected Letters is one to Archibald Henderson in which he calls attention to Clarence Rook's
sketch in the November 1896 Chap-Book. He en-
closed a copy with his letter to Henderson and added
with a modesty all his own: "This is one of the best
things of the kind ever done about me. "
The foregoing makes known the origin of Nine
Answers by G. Bernard Shaw but it does not explain
how the manuscript, which had never before been
published exactly as Shaw prepared it, came into
Mr. Kern's hands. It is a disarmingly candid, pug-
nacious but good-tempered revelation of Shaw's history and personality from his youth to success and
fame as a writer. In spite of a slight vein of prejudice running all through it, Christopher Morley's introduction is equally an appreciative and characteristically personal performance. In many ways it tells
more about Christopher Morley than it does about
Shaw.
The two men had much in common. Each sported
a fine grizzled beard relating them to the Elizabethans.
They were both professional writers and earned a
good livelihood from their writing. They possessed
varied literary talents and a gusty humor, and both
were brilliant talkers. They were to an unusual degree self-revealing in their writings: Shaw directly
with first person anecdotes concerning his personal
triumphs; Morley less obtrusively with the use of a
Doppelgänger device as in John Mistletoe and The
Man Who Made Friends with Himself. There the

comparison would seem to end. Poetry was Morley's first love; "I have never been completely happy except when writing verse"; Shaw exalted facts, left no poetry as a legacy of his love. Morley was above all a warm, human being; Shaw at birth was never completely incarnated as a human being. Morley was by no means a realist; by his own admission he chose the forms of fantasy and fable to spare himself the bitterness of facing the sad and ugly. Shaw put aside nothing, pleasant or unpleasant; as pointed out by a reviewer of his collected letters, "The impulse to realism and truth-telling ... made him acknowledge human unhappiness if only to be reasonable about it. "

Nine Answers by G. Bernard Shaw, even though a Shaw fragment and a minor one at that, bears witness not only to his paradoxical career and famous wit, but also to what Christopher Morley describes as "his cool exemption from passion. " By his own confession, Shaw was "hopelessly unnatural, and void of real passion"; his only asset being his intelligence and his learning. This apparently troubled Morley whose popularity was his unabashed humanity and sentimentality. In his introduction he likens Shaw to Henry Ford with his passion for "mechanical ingenuities. " A more apt comparison is suggested by an anonymous reviewer in the Times Literary Supplement who finds in Shaw's private letters "no self-revelations, no confessions, no dark doubts, no moments of despair or anger, indeed no passions at all. " After a while, he writes "Shaw begins to seem a bit inhuman, like the nightmare that Yeats had of him, as a smiling sewing machine. "

INTRODUCTION BY CHRISTOPHER MORLEY

to Shaw's
Nine Answers by G. Bernard Shaw

I have been wondering just what may be the moral of my having been asked by Jerome Kern to write a preface to this fragment in which Mr. Shaw holds the mirror up to Nurture; I conclude that it is all a part of the general hu-

morous Retributive Principle. For certainly not many have
had opportunity to write prefaces for Shaw: he gets too much
enjoyment out of doing it himself. Also it is agreeable to
record (Shaw having made us familiar with his vegetarian
tastes as he has with his hygienic undergarb, his morals,
manners, and everything else) that the persuasion to write
this preface would never have been consummated but for a
chicken-and-ham pie served by Mr. Mitchell Kennerley at the
Plaza--a slab of daintily tinted mosaic meats so beautifully
like the plan of a Roman Villa I once saw in the Cotswolds
that no carnal spirit could refuse to show its gratitude. I
hope that some day some shining hand will do justice to that
upholstered corner of the Plaza grillroom where Mitchell
Kennerley embarks his guests for victual. To see the Caliph
A. Edward Newton truncating a cocoanut pie, or Mr. Bliss
Carman tenderly contemplating the downward billowing whorls
of cream deflucted into a tall glass of iced coffee, or Mr.
Kern himself gaily incisive upon a nugget of Roquefort while
describing a first issue of Pickwick he has just bought--these
are small marginalia upon the pleasant comedy of Manhattan
that I find savorously enjoyable.

But about Shaw: I know no tribute to the man that is
more comprehensive than this, that I very early made up my
mind (merely instinctively) that I didn't need to bother about
him. About the year 1906, when I went to Haverford, the
small eastern colleges were in travail with undergraduate
performances of "Man and Superman." Then again, at Oxford a few years later, a small group of young Britons who
met once a week to read plays aloud, invited me in as a
collaborating mouthpiece in "Captain Brassbound's Conver-
sion." It was thought that I might be able to give an appropriate "American accent" to some character who appears in
that piece. Both these initiations, and a performance of
"Fanny's First Play" seen when it was first put on in London, were so excessively tedious to my delicate mind, that
I concluded Shaw was not for me. And, on the basis of
what evidence I had, I was quite right. I had also, very
young, tried to read "Mrs. Warren's Profession," having
somehow gathered the impression that it was scandalous.
All these attempts being complete failures, I concluded that
Shaw was a very dull and posturing fellow who had some
mysterious appeal for the ultraconscious intellectuals--a
class of whom I was already dumbly suspicious. What I did
not realize, and what is indeed the highest compliment to

Shaw's high-tension efficacy as a spark-coil was that already by that time--fifteen years ago--Shaw's ideas had so generally percolated into public unconsciousness that I was absorbing them all around me, without knowing their source.   Many a sophomore smartness, crudely ventilated in some petty college exercise, in a hundred or a thousand rustic academes, was the final buzz of an electric circuit originating in the dry cells of Shaw's mind twenty years before.

But I should probably have dismissed Mr. Shaw altogether, as not my meat (or my vegetable) if it had not been for a letter written before I was born--a letter written to William Archer by the great hero of my boyhood, R. L. S. This letter--which I hope all Shavians are familiar with, for it is a very shrewd comment on Shaw, vented by Stevenson on reading "Cashel Byron's Profession"--spoke so spiritedly, almost hysterically, of Shaw's gift and promise that I said to myself (with the composure of an undergraduate) that a man of whom R. L. S. could write with such excitement must, after all, have something in him.   Stevenson's formula for Shaw, after reading "Cashel Byron," was as follows:

1 part Charles Reade; 1 part Henry James or some kindred author badly assimilated; 1/2 part Disraeli (perhaps unconscious); 1 1/2 parts struggling, overlaid original talent; 1 part blooming, gaseous folly. That is the equation as it stands ... [L]et him beware of his damned century; his gifts of insane chivalry and animated narration are just those that might be slain and thrown out like an untimely birth by the Dæmon of the epoch.

Well, the Dæmon of the epoch did have its effect on G. B. S.   Whether for good or ill, it is too early to say. With his industry (as great as Trollope's), his seriousness (as intense as John Stuart Mill's), and his mad humor (as fierce as Meredith's), he might well--and if publishers had had half an eye, certainly would--have gone on in a series of novels that would have been unlike anything in the course of British fiction.   No one can read "The Man of Destiny," for instance, without saying, What a short story gone astray! No one can read "Cashel Byron's Profession" (no one but a publisher, at any rate) without seeing its extraordinary charm, humor, and subtle spoofing.   (I wish Mr. Shaw, who is so legitimately interested in all details of his own career, would dig up somehow the original Readers' Reports on that book when it was offered for publication. Having had some experience in the comedy of Publishers' Readers myself, I should love to know what they said about it. No one can read "An Unsocial Socialist" ... but I don't believe anyone can read it at all.

After 1776, there was hardly another such important social event in the strictly English-spoken world until 1876, when Shaw--breaking away from his beginning as a realtor!-- ascended upon London. Nothing, of course, could permanently impede the worldly success of so unworldly a creature. He had frugality, he had impudence, he had industry and a grue- some certainty of the importance of being flip. He made (he tells us) £6 in nine years; but whatever he made, he lived on it. Finally he horned in--the phrase is accurate, for it was as "Corno di Bassetto" that he made his first serious dents in the public pachyderm. And wherever sheer intelli- gence is esteemed--intelligence as a living rational force, apart from sentiment, charity, convention, modesty, or any of the usual concessions to opinion--the name of Shaw is honorable. That is not to say that I, or you, or anyone else, honors it in the highest degree: but it is honorable. It will never be popular, for intelligence is not a popular quality.

Mr. Shaw has long since outlived the old silly repute of being a buffoon, an Eulenspiegel. In this document which Mr. Kern reprints, he tells us his tactic--"My method is to take the utmost trouble to find the right thing to say, and then to say it with the utmost levity." The difficulty is that his grim social earnestness hardly permits him to be skittish enough. We have then the distressing spectacle of a social philosopher compelled--or believing himself compelled--to write plays which are very little read (and by many consid- ered unreadable) for the sake of barbing them with prefaces which are violently important. What is the fatality that con- demns everything of Shaw's, unless ballasted with a play, to mere hole-and-corner circulation? The brilliant and delight- ful essay "On Going to Church" is not included in his col- lected volumes: it is only accessible (so far as I know) in the linoleum vest-pocket format of the "Little Leather Li- brary" or in the villainously printed pamphlet of the mysteri- ous Haldeman-Julius. It was, indeed, once pirated by Elbert Hubbard: but why not a legitimated issue? For this Shaw, long suspected as antichrist (his beard, his subfusc garment-

ing, and the Passover cranks of his diet lending plausibility
to the myth) is one of the most truly religious men of our
time.   It might have been of him and Christianity that the
traditional story-beginning was invented--"There was an
Irishman and he said to a Jew...."

Shaw has remarked that there is nothing interesting to
be said about him that he has not already said about himself.
I believe it to be true.   I merely wish to suggest my own
private meditation that there is much in common between him
and Henry Ford.   Shaw has told us somewhere of his passion
for mechanical ingenuities, and that he once nearly bought a
cash register, fascinated by its automatic punctilio, though
he had no earthly use for it.   (The mental picture, also, of
Shaw on his motor-bike, speeding down English roads with
sandy beard bifurcated in the breeze, is one that stimulates
me.)   Perhaps, likewise, in his resolute focus upon practical
human welfare, his personal simplicity and kindness, his instinctive suspicion of mass-pivoted ideas, his cool business
sense and rejection of fuzbuz and doctrine, his boyish and
often most irritating prankish humor, there are kinsprit traits.
Perhaps if we can imagine a Henry Ford endowed with literary
genius, we shall have a clearer notion of Shaw.

For it boils down to this at the last, that the rarest
and most troublesome spiritual resource is pure unadulterated
reasonableness, good sense.   The sanity and clear slogging
logic of Shaw's ideas, his cool exemption from passion, are
horrifying to many.   His preface to "Getting Married," for
instance, contains the gist of practically all the novels that
have made a sensation in the past fifteen years.   I haven't
read any of A. S. M. Hutchinson's best-sellers, but I venture that the essential calories of all such fictions are tucked
away in the meaty ribs of this amazing document.   It is a
Magna Charta of personal, social, and political morality; yet
one reads it with a kind of sorry despair, suspecting that not
in three hundred years will society as a whole attain so
shrewdly purged and reasonable a view toward perplexing
matters.   It contains wisdom of the pungent and nipping sort
that people laboriously accumulate only after gruelling experience.   Yet, as a piece of what the textbooks call "exposition" it is hardly a success.   Shaw's characteristic quality--
which he learned, he says, partly from Samuel Butler--is
that of stating truth with such gusto, plainness and startling
humor that the gentle reader is appalled.   That quality is

sometimes called bluntness, and sometimes sharpness: but whichever name you prefer, the plainer sort of folk ("journalists and bishops and American presidents and other simple people, " as Shaw puts it) are either stunned or wounded. The general public have little appetite for truth unless they believe it to be fiction.

There are other things to be said; but even a preface to Shaw must have an end. There is a certain vegetarian quality in Shaw's mind, a lack of gravy, a pallor, a nunlike cleanliness. He is fond of saying that if he had been born in 1556 instead of 1856, he would have given Shakespeare a run for his money. But if Shaw had been an Elizabethan instead of a Victorian he would have had to roll his bread-crust in the red juices of the roast. There were fewer vegetables served at the Mermaid. The faculty that one misses in him, I think, and the faculty that is essential for any dramatist of world-stature, is the poetic. He never averts his eyes from facts. He is as humorous as a man can be, but is he mad enough? The mere fact that such a question can be asked shows that we have travelled since the Nineties, when Shaw seemed to some (one gathers) a bedlamite from the yonder moon. But we should not have made that transit unless his ideas had been motive. Yet his madness seems now a sane and reasonable kind of lunacy.

If a man will be sufficiently odd in England, he can easily become fashionable in America. If there is one thing in the world that Shaw takes completely seriously, it is probably the United States. And with that pure and serene sagacity that has always been his, he has refrained from testing this One Illusion by observation. I had suspected that he would really have come over to see Dempsey fight. But I begin to hope he will not come, for any reason. He is a great man: and if he never comes here to see for himself the most curiously exhilarating of all social comedies, American democracy, he may safely be put down as a Genius. I myself regard him as a great novelist gone wrong. By all the rules, he should long ago have grown embittered: for forty years he has been telling us pure wisdom, and the world is unaltered. He must be, himself, one of the most lovable of men. I will do almost anything for him, except read his plays.

CHRISTOPHER MORLEY

ALLAN NEVINS

Shortly after John F. Kennedy graduated from Harvard in 1940, he served as a PT boat commander in the South Pacific. Severely wounded during a night engagement with an enemy destroyer, he was twice decorated by the Navy for bravery and leadership. He served in the United States House of Representatives and later in the Senate before his election to the presidency.

While convalescing from a serious spinal operation in mid-January 1955, the junior senator from Massachusetts had a great deal of time on his hands. He undertook to read and write about the careers of leaders in American political life who had displayed "that most admirable of human virtues--courage." As his friend and biographer, Theodore Sorenson, observes, "the work was a tonic to his spirits and a distraction from pain." The fortunate result of this convalescent period was a book entitled Profiles in Courage in which the Senator tells the stories of ten or more legislators and political leaders who displayed conspicuous courage by championing a course of action which they knew to be unpopular, but which they believed to be in the national interest.

In an epilogue to his book, Senator Kennedy clearly implies that he is aiming at the general reader when he writes: "These problems do not even concern politics alone--for the same basic choice of courage or compliance continually faces us all, whether we fear the anger of constituents, friends, a board of directors of our union, whenever we stand against the flow of opinion on strongly contested issues." His faith was fully justified.

124

The book became an immediate and consistent best-
seller. Certainly, it is equally clear that Profiles
in Courage is intended for readers with a more
specialized interest in history--in short, for the historian. Here, Kennedy the amateur, was entering
the field of the professional. He needed someone to
bless his history. He turned to the old master, Allan Nevins, the distinguished professor of American
history at Columbia University. The professor was
amenable and, in an enthusiastic foreword, let the
world know that Profiles in Courage is good history.

FOREWORD BY ALLAN NEVINS

to John F. Kennedy's
Profiles in Courage

As John Bright once said, men are not great statesmen merely because they happen to have held great offices.
They must present better title deeds to eminence, of which
courage is one. Senator Kennedy treats of a special kind of
courage: the moral courage of a parliamentary leader who
in behalf of principle confronts the passion of colleagues,
constituents and a majority of the general public. His examples, chosen from the history of the American Congress
and mainly the Senate, are striking, varied and memorable;
he puts into his narration a fine mastery of the psychology
of the different periods described, as well as of the facts in
each drama; and he makes his whole book so absorbing that
most readers will race through it, fully comprehending only
at the end the lesson in civic virtue which it enforces.   Indeed, this volume teaches so much in history, in practical
politics and in sound morals, all bound together, that it con-
stitutes a real public service.

Courage, as Senator Kennedy explains in his first
chapter, is a diamond with many facets, and it owes much
to its setting. It is not always a simple trait, for motiva-
tions are often complex; and in the rough and tumble of political life, with its heavy pressures, its demands for honest
compromise, and its constant presentation of second-best
choices, courage can seldom be manifested in simple ways.
The right course is not always clear. "These are days of

special perplexity and depression, " wrote Grover Cleveland
in 1894, "and the path of public duty is unusually rugged. "
Perplexity!--that is a word which many a true statesman
would echo.   Even Washington, even Lincoln, were not always sure in just what direction their courage should be directed.   Greeley wished Lincoln to be courageous about
emancipation, for example, at a time when such intrepidity
would have been decidedly premature.   So much depends, in
measuring courage, as well as other political virtues, upon
the point of view!   When Richard Bland of free-silver fame
once exploded in the House, apropos of opposition measures
of uncommon hardihood and nerve, "This is downright filibustering, " the Republican leader Thomas B. Reed retorted:
"Downright?   You mean upright. "

One great merit of this volume is that its instances
of courage are all true, clear, and in the last analysis constructive; its heroes--John Quincy Adams, Webster, Houston,
Ross of Kansas, George Norris--all exercised their courage
in a noble way for large ends.   A considerable ingredient of
courage is necessarily bound up in the nature of fanatics,
like the Northern Abolitionists and the Southern fire-eaters
in days before the Civil War; but this is not a type of courage we can greatly admire.   The distinction between true
courage and fanatic courage was well implied in George Fris-
bie Hoar's characterization of Charles Sumner, who professed
to subject every measure to the test of moral law: "Where
duty seemed to Sumner to utter its high commands, he could
see no obstacle in hostile majorities and no restraint in the
limitations of a hostile Constitution. "   What is the use of
courage that flouts the Constitution?   Another false kind of
courage is that which springs from a hopelessly erratic temperament.   John Randolph of Roanoke showed great bravery
in opposing the War of 1812; he was dauntless always, brilliant often; but he was so fretful, unreasonable, abusive, and
wrongheaded that his courage ran to waste.   Equally unim-
pressive is the courage of the inveterate objector.   Senator
George Edmunds of Vermont was such a man; it was said
that if he was the only person in the world, George would
object to everything that Edmunds proposed.

Mr. Kennedy's instances are of a different kind, the
courage of intelligent, farsighted, reasonable men anxious to
hold the ship of state to its true course.   John Quincy Adams
broke with his party and State to sustain the nation's honor in

the Embargo crisis; later he faced a storm of hatred to vindicate the right of petition.   Daniel Webster knew that half of his party and nearly all of New England--including poets and essayists whose words would sting like serpents--would spurn him if he espoused Clay's great Compromise; but he unflinchingly rose to deliver his Seventh of March speech. So the story goes.

It is an interesting fact that so many of Senator Kennedy's instances show us a parliamentary leader proclaiming his independence of his erring constituency.   From the beginnings of parliamentary government in Western Europe one common weakness appeared on which many nascent legislatures foundered.   Almost all the various assemblies of estates were formed of self-armed aristocratic groups, quite as jealous of their rights and privileges as of their duties.   This was true of England, Scotland, France, Castile, Scandinavia, and later Prussia.   The constituent groups naturally regarded their representatives as so many attorneys to protect their interests.   Unwilling to give them full freedom of deliberation and action, they fettered these representatives by the strictest instructions or mandates.   In France, such rigid delegation of powers, such a requirement that every deputy must battle for the privileges of his group or order, was one of the factors which finally precipitated the Revolution.   Happily for England, there a strong feeling of the unity of the realm, and the importance of legislating for all instead of a part, modified the situation.   Parliamentary independence of constituents grew strong, and the tradition was inherited by America. For both countries, Burke's famous address to the electors of Bristol became the classic statement of the freedom of the elected representative to exercise his own best judgment. Senator Ross, defying outraged Kansas to vote against the ousting of Andrew Johnson from the Presidency, was carrying out Burke's principle and maintaining the finest standards of Anglo-American legislative bodies.

Sporadic instances of courage on isolated and unimportant issues have no great significance.   To be important, courage must be exhibited in behalf of some large cause or rule.   John Stuart Mill made a brave fight in Parliament against the martial law cruelties of Governor Eyre in Jamaica. He did it, as he points out in his autobiography, not from a mere feeling of humanitarian sympathy with maltreated Negroes, but to maintain the sacred principle that British subjects everywhere were under the rule of civil law, not of military license. Senator Foraker, bravely intervening on behalf of the 160-odd Negro troopers dishonorably dismissed from the service after the Brownsville Affair, declared that he also was defending a greater cause than that of a few soldiers; the cause of a fair trial. Throughout our Congressional history, adherence to principle has fortunately had repeated and spectacular illustration. Numerous instances might be added to those selected by Senator Kennedy, from Calhoun's opposition to the war with Mexico (so popular in his own section) to certain brave acts of Senator Vandenberg--who, incidentally, possessed sufficient courage to admit wholeheartedly that he had been wrong on the great issue of isolation.

How courageous, for example, was the course of Senator Stephen A. Douglas on the Lecompton Constitution! Douglas was a Democrat; he was a close friend of many Southerners; he had been unswervingly loyal to the Buchanan Administration; he cared little about slavery. The Administration, almost the whole South, and a heavy majority of his Democratic colleagues in the Senate stood for admitting Kansas as the fifteenth slave state under the Lecompton instrument. But this Constitution had been written by a small proslavery rump convention after Kansas had declared for free soil by a tremendous popular majority. To Douglas a cardinal principle was at stake--the principle that American citizens have the right to make their own institutions; and though every conceivable pressure was brought to bear, every threat, every cajolery, he stood firm for his doctrine of popular sovereignty. He knew that he was almost certainly casting away all his golden chances for the Presidency; but he put aside the thought. He was illustrating in a matter of the largest moment the kind of courageous integrity which William A. Wheeler (in time Vice-President under Hayes) expressed in a colloquy with Senator Conkling.

Said Roscoe Conkling: "Wheeler, if you will act with us, there is nothing in the gift of the State of New York to which you may not reasonably aspire." Conkling was practically boss of New York. Replied Wheeler: "Mr. Conkling, there is nothing in the gift of the State of New York which will compensate me for the forfeiture of my self-respect."

Particularly interesting is Senator Kennedy's chapter

on George Norris, who with Senator Robert M. La Follette--
"Fighting Bob"--displayed a specially constructive kind of
courage. Bryce remarked in his American Commonwealth
that this was peculiarly rare in American legislative bodies.
"The American statesman is apt to be timid in advocacy as
well as infantile in suggestion. " Mr. Kennedy gives us some
reasons for thinking that the kind of courage which goes into
the leadership of good measures rather than opposition to bad
ones is increasing. He speaks frankly of the changed re-
quirements as to courage. Since Bryce's day, pressure
groups have become more numerous, better organized, and
far more powerful. Now that the merger of the A. F. of L.
and the C. I. O. has been achieved, labor is as strong as
business--and business is highly organized, highly self-con-
scious. The farmer, his five or six million families controlling many broad States politically, is also powerful; and
these three groups but begin the list. Senator Kennedy has
some interesting things to say about the possibility of putting
courage into the guidance, rather than the mere defeat, of
special interests--for many interests have legitimate aims.
He suggests that Members of the House and Senate have more
expert wisdom than of old. Norris, at any rate, had the
combined courage and wisdom that kept fighting hard on the
farm-relief and public power issues when others were trying
to form the battle line on the false issues of prohibition and
religion.

Moral courage is great and admirable in itself; but it
must be pointed out that it almost never appears except as
part of that greater entity called character. A man without
character may give fitful exhibitions of courage, as even
Aaron Burr did when in the disputed election of 1800 he refused to bargain with the willing Federalists for the Presidency. But no man without character is consistently courageous, just as no man of real character is lacking in consistent courage. In short, moral courage is allied with the
other traits which make up character: honesty, deep seriousness, a firm sense of principle, candor, resolution.

It is an indisputable fact that in governmental affairs
the American people value character more than they do intellect: that they are indeed a little distrustful of intellectual
subtlety or cleverness unless assured that character underlies
it. In this wise attitude they are like other English-speaking
peoples. Perhaps the most shining example of courage in a

legislative capacity to be found in all history is that of John
Hampden, so much admired by Theodore Roosevelt.   He had
an efficient intelligence and a great talent for dispatching
business.   But it was to his moral rather than his intellectual qualities that he owed his vast influence.   He was above
all, as Macaulay says, a man of character.   As the historian
Clarendon, writing of the Long Parliament, puts it: "I am
persuaded that his power and interest at that time were
greater to do good or hurt than any man's in the kingdom...;
for his reputation of honesty was universal, and his affec-
tions seemed so publicly guided, that no corrupt or private
ends could bias them."   In the same way, it was Washington's supreme gifts of character rather than of mind, which
carried us through the Revolution; and it was the very different gifts of character in Lincoln which maintained the nation's unity in the Civil War.   In any Senator or Representative, courage will spring not as an independent trait but from
the nurture of moral breadth and poise.

We may add that before there can be much character
and courage in Congress, there must be a great deal of it
in the American people.   We shall look in vain for these
treasures in Washington if they are not scattered widely
everywhere from Boston to San Diego.   Wrote Lord Bryce:
"America is all of a piece; its institutions are the product
of its economic and social conditions, and the expression of
its character."   That is, democracy--sound democracy--is
not a cause, but an effect.   Our national character will determine whether our legislators will be courageous or coward-
ly, and our politics good or bad.   This is a fact which we
may read between the lines of Senator Kennedy's admirable
book.   At times, as he notes, the bad has gotten the upper
hand in Congress and in much of the country--notably just
after the Civil War; but these lapses have been transient.
We may hope that Americans will continue to exhibit principle, moderation, orderliness and justice as abiding traits,
with the courage to defend them when attacked; if they do,
the national Legislature will also exhibit them.

--ALLAN NEVINS

A. EDWARD NEWTON

The first of Charles Dickens's books for the Christmas trade, A Christmas Carol, written when he was not quite thirty-two years old, is as immortally associated with the Yuletide spirit as steaming plum pudding, sizzling turkey, snow-covered fields, and families gathered indoors around the Christmas tree. Thackeray described it as "a national benefit, and to every man or woman who reads it a personal kindness." Indeed, it is so symbolic of Christmas that Dickens is sometimes spoken of as The Man Who Invented Christmas.

In another part of the world, a generation later, there flashed on the literary horizon a man named A. Edward Newton (familiarly known as A. E. N.) who wrote a book which had a great deal to say about London and Dickens's books and caused a sensation among booklovers everywhere. The book was entitled The Amenities of Book-Collecting and it had to do with A. E. N.'s experiences in London and at home in book collecting. His wise literary judgment and wide acquaintance with prominent collectors and booksellers made the book fast, absorbing reading. Christopher Morley referred to it as "the A. B. C. (The Amenities of Book Collecting) of high spirits in print." Newton's friend, the great book-collector A. S. W. Rosenbach, said that A. E. N. did more for book-collecting in this country than any other writer, and he referred to the first quarter of this century as the "Age of Newton." In one of Newton's books there is a photograph showing the author in his famous "Oak Knoll" library housed in his Main Line country estate near Philadelphia--a chubby little man in a checkered suit. He is posing with Miss Agnes

131

Repplier, who is pouring tea from Dr. Johnson's teapot, while in the background his friend Professor Charles Osgood of Princeton stands nonchalantly against a book-lined wall case, beside which a Reynolds portrait of the great Johnson appears to be looking down benignly on the tea party.

A. E. N. spent a great deal of his time in London, which offered much in the way of book exploration in the first quarter of the century. Few men knew or loved the city more than he did. It was the best place, he writes in his preface, to read A Christmas Carol on Christmas eve. It was not surprising that Ellery Sedgwick should be able to persuade him to write a preface for the Carol when the Atlantic Monthly Press brought out a new edition in 1920. In his preface he reminisces about some of the prize Dickens items in his collection, including several presentation copies given by Dickens to his friends. If he could have one wish as a literary man, he once said, it would be to write "another and a better Christmas Carol." Well, the good fairy vanished before he got his wish, but at least he had the privilege of writing a preface to his favorite Christmas book.

INTRODUCTION BY A. EDWARD NEWTON

to Charles Dickens's
A Christmas Carol

"Are you running a corner in 'Christmas Carols'?" a friend inquired the other evening, as he stood facing my book-shelves, looking at a little cluster of books in brown cloth jackets. "No, not exactly," I answered, "but that book has been a favorite for a lifetime; indeed, with the exception of the manuscript, which is safely locked up in the Pierpont Morgan Library, I admit to having a very pretty 'run' of 'Carols,' including a presentation copy, with an inscription reading, 'Thomas Beard, from his old friend Charles Dickens.'"

The manuscript of the "Carol," so rewritten, interlined, and corrected as to be almost illegible, except to one

A. EDWARD NEWTON

accustomed to Dickens's handwriting, is far from being Mr. Morgan's chief literary possession; but it is an ornament to any collection, and Miss Greene, who showed it to me not long ago, told me that it is one of the items that almost all visitors wish to see.

Contrasting small things with great, I have in my own Dickens collection the original drawing by John Leech of "The Last of the Spirits, " which I was lucky enough to pick up in a New York bookshop a few years ago, and I am still seeking the original drawing of Mr. Fezziwig's Ball. It must be in existence somewhere; who has it? It is the gayest little picture in all the world, and fairly exudes Christmas cheer. Who would not love to dance a Sir Roger de Coverly with Mrs. Fezziwig, her face one vast substantial smile?

We hear much of the world being shaken from centre to circumference by this or that evil influence; influences for good are not so dramatic in their operation, but they are of greater duration, and among them Dickens's "Christmas Carol" ranks high. It is the best book of its kind in the world. I am confirmed in this opinion by Dickens's friend, Lord Jeffrey, who said that it had done more good than all the pulpits in Christendom. Thackeray referred to it as a national benefit, and with the passage of time the English-speaking world has grown to look upon it as an international blessing.

The first edition of this famous book appeared a few days before Christmas, 1843, and six thousand copies were sold the first day. It appeared when the vogue for "colored plate" books was at its height; but from the figures given by Forster, Dickens's biographer, it would seem that no care had been taken by the publishers to discover what the cost of manufacture would be before the selling price was fixed. No expense was spared to make it a beautiful little book. It was daintily printed, and tastefully bound in cloth, with gilt edges, and Leech had supplied drawings for four full-page engraved illustrations which were subsequently exquisitely colored by hand, and in addition there were four small woodcuts from the same artist. But when the financial returns came in, Dickens was terribly disappointed. He had been led to expect that he would receive a thousand pounds, whereas there was a profit of but two hundred and thirty. However, the second and third editions brought the profits up to over

seven hundred and twenty-odd pounds, and countless other
editions followed, so that in the end the profits were considerable; but it was Dickens's first and last experience with
"colored plates."

John C. Eckel, the accepted authority on first editions
of Dickens, says that the "Carol" has just enough "bibliographical twists" to make it interesting.   An ardent collector
could master them in ten minutes.   The title-page of the
first issue of the first edition should be printed in <u>red</u> <u>and</u>
<u>blue</u>; the date must be 1843; and Stave I, on page <u>one</u>, should
have the numeral "I," and not be spelled out, "one," as it
was in the second issue.   Moreover, the "end-papers," that
is to say, the papers pasted down inside the covers, should
be of a Paris green color and not a pale lemon yellow.   I
bought such a copy thirty years ago for thirty shillings, and
sold it a few years later, when I was hard up, for fifteen
dollars; such a copy is now worth thirty pounds if in fine
condition, whereas a copy lacking these points is worth only
a few dollars.

A few, a very few copies were issued with the title-
page in <u>red</u> <u>and</u> <u>green</u>, with the lemon end-papers, and
"Stave I," bearing the date 1844.   These were evidently trial
pages, and the green border was abandoned in favor of a
border printed in blue.   On account of their great scarcity,
these red-and-green "Carols" are much more costly--I forget what I paid for mine.   Charles Sessler, the Philadelphia
bookseller, who specializes in Dickens, tells me that $450
would not be high for a really fine copy.   Charles Plumptre
Johnson, in his "Hints to Dickens Collectors," says, "I have
in my possession a copy, <u>absolutely</u> uncut, which I believe
to be the first copy printed and sent to the binder for his
guidance."   Oh, joy!   Oh, joy!

Not everyone can read the book as it ought to be
read, as I have frequently read it, on Christmas Eve in
London; but it is a book which should be read, if not in an
early edition, at least in such a <u>format</u> as, reader, the one
you hold in your hand.   I have always resented this book being got up in modern fashion, however beautifully illustrated,
printed, and bound; nor should it be read in a large volume
out of a "set," or expensively bound in leather.   No, as my
friend Dr. Johnson has said, "a book that can be held easily
in the hand and carried to the fireside is the most useful

after all, " and this is especially true of the "Carol, " which is a fireside book, if there ever was one.   Originally it sold for five shillings, but this was almost eighty years ago, and shillings went further in those days than dollars do to-day. I have no idea what the price of this book will be, but whatever it is, buy it: buy two copies of it, one to give away and one to read, as the season rolls around.   And when you come to know it, by heart almost, so that it begins to sing the moment you turn its pages, you will come to love the music of this Carol, and in the spirit of Christmas will exclaim, with Tiny Tim: "God Bless Us, Every One. "

A.   EDWARD NEWTON.

"OAK KNOLL, "
Daylesford, Penna. , September 2, 1920.

Stephen Crane, who had no personal knowledge
of battle, produced his small classic The Red Badge
of Courage when he was only twenty-two years of age.
His hero was not an officer but an inarticulate young
recruit fresh from the farm.   The soldier boy waited
and wondered, listened to conflicting camp rumors,
ran away in his first engagement but returned to
fight again so bravely that he won high praise from
his commanding officer--this was the story.
Although poorly rewarded monetarily, Crane's
reputation in his own time was considerable after
the publication of his masterpiece, and his output
rose.   In the remaining five years of his short life
--he died at the age of twenty-eight--he wrote jour-
nalistic sketches about the Spanish-American war, a
satirical novel about a war correspondent in the
Greco-Turkish war, two volumes of verse, a collection of tales about childhood days in a small New
York town, and numerous short stories which were
collected and published in book form.   During his
last years he lived in rural England where he was
very much appreciated and enjoyed the company of
such congenial neighbors as Conrad, Wells, and
Hueffer.   In the last months of his life he went to
Germany for a rest cure where he died of tuberculosis.
Interest in Stephen Crane seems to surface whenever the United States is engaged in war.   Following
World War I, Vincent Starrett, a well-known Chicago
critic and Crane's first bibliographer, edited a Modern Library edition of his short stories and sketches,
entitled Men, Women and Boats.   Of this collection,
the American author Louis Zara wrote "Thomas Beer,

136

John Berryman, and others, like myself, would
probably never have followed with Crane studies but
for an early revival of Starrett." The writings of
Stephen Crane which Vincent Starrett gathers together in this volume are full of good yarns and
dialogue, dipping and wandering off into a variety of
side roads including impressions of London and a
lively essay on "The Scotch Express." Of the stories, "The Open Boat" has remained lastingly popular. Starrett speaks of it as "perhaps his [Crane's]
finest piece of work." The impressions of London
are a series of vignettes, gay and humorous, afford-
ing glimpses of buses, stations, streets, cabmen,
porters, and policemen. "I did not then care to see
the Thames Embankment nor the Houses of Parliament. I considered the porter and the cabman to be
more important," he wrote. While no selection of
Crane's verse appears in the collection, Starrett
speaks of his poetry and quotes several poems in
his introduction. Crane's poetry was not of great
volume and not all he wrote is up to the level of
the poems quoted in the introduction, but Starrett
makes the point that Crane was a pioneer in the
free verse and Imagist movement, a view confirmed
by Carl Sandburg in his Letters to Dead Imagists.
Even more important, Starrett's edition of Men,
Women and Boats, and his long introduction, help
to dispel the notion that Stephen Crane was a one-
book author and to show the wide range of Stephen
Crane's literary and artistic talents.

"Stephen Crane: An Estimate"
AN INTRODUCTION BY VINCENT STARRETT

to Stephen Crane's
Men, Women and Boats

It hardly profits us to conjecture what Stephen Crane
might have written about the World War had he lived. Certainly, he would have been in it, in one capacity or another.
No man had a greater talent for war and personal adventure,
nor a finer art in describing it. Few writers of recent
times could so well describe the poetry of motion as mani-

fested in the surge and flow of battle, or so well depict the isolated deed of heroism in its stark simplicity and terror.

To such an undertaking as Henri Barbusse's "Under Fire," that powerful, brutal book, Crane would have brought an analytical genius almost clairvoyant. He possessed an uncanny vision; a descriptive ability photographic in its clarity and its care for minutiae--yet unphotographic in that the big central thing often is omitted, to be felt rather than seen in the occult suggestion of detail. Crane would have seen and depicted the grisly horror of it all, as did Barbusse, but also he would have seen the glory and the ecstasy and the wonder of it, and over that his poetry would have been spread.

While Stephen Crane was an excellent psychologist, he was also a true poet. Frequently his prose was finer poetry than his deliberate essays in poesy. His most famous book, "The Red Badge of Courage," is essentially a psychological study, a delicate clinical dissection of the soul of a recruit, but it is also a tour de force of the imagination. When he wrote the book he had never seen a battle: he had to place himself in the situation of another. Years later, when he came out of the Greco-Turkish fracas, he remarked to a friend: "'The Red Badge' is all right."

Written by a youth who had scarcely passed his majority, this book has been compared with Tolstoy's "Sebastopol" and Zola's "La Débâcle," and with some of the short stories of Ambrose Bierce. The comparison with Bierce's work is legitimate; with the other books, I think, less so. Tolstoy and Zola see none of the traditional beauty of battle; they apply themselves to a devoted--almost obscene--study of corpses and carnage generally; and they lack the American's instinct for the rowdy commonplace, the natural, the irreverent, which so materially aids his realism. In "The Red Badge of Courage" invariably the tone is kept down where one expects a height: the most heroic deeds are accomplished with studied awkwardness.

Crane was an obscure free-lance when he wrote this book. The effort, he says, somewhere, "was born of pain-- despair, almost." It was a better piece of work, however, for that very reason, as Crane knew. It is far from flawless. It has been remarked that it bristles with as many grammatical errors as with bayonets; but it is a big canvas, and I am certain that many of Crane's deviations from the rules of polite rhetoric were deliberate experiments, looking to effect--effect which, frequently, he gained.

Stephen Crane "arrived" with this book.   There are, of course, many who never have heard of him, to this day, but there was a time when he was very much talked of. That was in the middle nineties, following publication of "The Red Badge of Courage, " although even before that he had occasioned a brief flurry with his weird collection of poems called "The Black Riders and Other Lines. "   He was highly praised, and highly abused and laughed at; but he seemed to be "made. "   We have largely forgotten since.   It is a way we have.

Personally, I prefer his short stories to his novels and his poems; those, for instance, contained in "The Open Boat, " in "Wounds in the Rain, " and in "The Monster. "   The title-story in that first collection is perhaps his finest piece of work.   Yet what is it?   A truthful record of an adventure of his own in the filibustering days that preceded our war with Spain; the faithful narrative of the voyage of an open boat, manned by a handful of shipwrecked men.   But Captain Bligh's account of his small boat journey, after he had been sent adrift by the mutineers of the Bounty, seems tame in comparison, although of the two the English sailor's voyage was the more perilous.

In "The Open Boat" Crane again gains his effects by keeping down the tone where another writer might have attempted "fine writing" and have been lost.   In it perhaps is most strikingly evident the poetic cadences of his prose: its rhythmic, monotonous flow is the flow of the gray water that laps at the sides of the boat, that rises and recedes in cruel waves, "like little pointed rocks. "   It is a desolate picture, and the tale is one of our greatest short stories.   In the other tales that go to make up the volume are wild, exotic glimpses of Latin-America.   I doubt whether the color and spirit of that region have been better rendered than in Stephen Crane's curious, distorted, staccato sentences.

"War Stories" is the laconic sub-title of "Wounds in the Rain. "   It was not war on a grand scale that Crane saw in the Spanish-American complication, in which he participated as a war correspondent; no such war as the recent

139

horror.   But the occasions for personal heroism were no fewer than always, and the opportunities for the exercise of such powers of trained and appreciative understanding and sympathy as Crane possessed, were abundant.   For the most part, these tales are episodic, reports of isolated instances-- the profanely humorous experiences of correspondents, the magnificent courage of signalmen under fire, the forgotten adventure of a converted yacht--but all are instinct with the red fever of war, and are backgrounded with the choking smoke of battle.   Never again did Crane attempt the large canvas of "The Red Badge of Courage."   Before he had seen war, he imagined its immensity and painted it with the fury and fidelity of a Verestchagin; when he was its familiar, he singled out its minor, crimson passages for briefer but no less careful delineation.

In this book, again, his sense of the poetry of motion is vividly evident.   We see men going into action, wave on wave, or in scattering charges; we hear the clink of their ac- coutrements and their breath whistling through their teeth. They are not men going into action at all, but men going about their business, which at the moment happens to be the capture of a trench.   They are neither heroes nor cowards. Their faces reflect no particular emotion save, perhaps, a desire to get somewhere.   They are a line of men running for a train, or following a fire engine, or charging a trench. It is a relentless picture, ever changing, ever the same. But it contains poetry, too, in rich, memorable passages.

In "The Monster and Other Stories," there is a tale called "The Blue Hotel."   A Swede, its central figure, toward the end manages to get himself murdered.   Crane's descrip- tion of it is just as casual as that.   The story fills a dozen pages of the book; but the social injustice of the whole world is hinted in that space; the upside-downness of creation, right prostrate, wrong triumphant,--a mad, crazy world. The incident of the murdered Swede is just part of the back- wash of it all, but it is an illuminating fragment.   The Swede was slain, not by the gambler whose knife pierced his thick hide: he was the victim of a condition for which he was no more to blame than the man who stabbed him. Stephen Crane thus speaks through the lips of one of the characters:--

'We are all in it!   This poor gambler isn't even a

noun. He is a kind of an adverb. Every sin is the result of a collaboration. We, five of us, have collaborated in the murder of this Swede. Usually there are from a dozen to forty women really involved in every murder, but in this case it seems to be only five men--you, I, Johnnie, old Scully, and that fool of an unfortunate gambler came merely as a culmination, the apex of a human movement, and gets all the punishment. '

And then this typical and arresting piece of irony:--

'The corpse of the Swede, alone in the saloon, had its eyes fixed upon a dreadful legend that dwelt atop of the cash-machine: "This registers the amount of your purchase. "'

In "The Monster, " the ignorance, prejudice and cruelty of an entire community are sharply focussed. The realism is painful; one blushes for mankind. But while this story really belongs in the volume called "Whilomville Stories, " it is properly left out of that series. The Whilomville stories are pure comedy, and "The Monster" is a hideous tragedy.

Whilomville is any obscure little village one may happen to think of. To write of it with such sympathy and understanding, Crane must have done some remarkable listening in Boyville. The truth is, of course, he was a boy himself-- "a wonderful boy, " somebody called him--and was possessed of the boy mind. These tales are chiefly funny because they are so true--boy stories written for adults; a child, I suppose, would find them dull. In none of his tales is his curious understanding of human moods and emotions better shown.

A stupid critic once pointed out that Crane, in his search for striking effects, had been led into "frequent neglect of the time-hallowed rights of certain words, " and that in his pursuit of color he "falls occasionally into almost ludicrous mishap. " The smug pedantry of the quoted lines is sufficient answer to the charges, but in support of these assertions the critic quoted certain passages and phrases. He objected to cheeks "scarred" by tears, to "dauntless" statues, and to "terror-stricken" wagons. The very touches of poetic impressionism that largely make for Crane's greatness, are cited to prove him an ignoramus. There is the

141

finest of poetic imagery in the suggestions subtly conveyed by Crane's tricky adjectives, the use of which was as deliberate with him as his choice of a subject. But Crane was an imagist before our modern imagists were known.

This unconventional use of adjectives is marked in the Whilomville tales. In one of them Crane refers to the "solemn odor of burning turnips." It is the most nearly perfect characterization of burning turnips conceivable: can anyone improve upon that "solemn odor"?

Stephen Crane's first venture was "Maggie: A Girl of the Streets." It was, I believe, the first hint of naturalism in American letters. It was not a best-seller; it offers no solution of life; it is an episodic bit of slum fiction, ending with the tragic finality of a Greek drama. It is a skeleton of a novel rather than a novel, but it is a powerful outline, written about a life Crane had learned to know as a newspaper reporter in New York. It is a singularly fine piece of analysis, or a bit of extraordinarily faithful reporting, as one may prefer; but not a few French and Russian writers have failed to accomplish in two volumes what Crane achieved in two hundred pages. In the same category is "George's Mother," a triumph of inconsequential detail piling up with a cumulative effect quite overwhelming.

Crane published two volumes of poetry--"The Black Riders" and "War is Kind." Their appearance in print was jeeringly hailed; yet Crane was only pioneering in the free verse that is to-day, if not definitely accepted, at least more than tolerated. I like the following love poem as well as any rhymed and conventionally metrical ballad that I know:--

> Should the wide world roll away,
> Leaving black terror,
> Limitless night,
> Nor God, nor man, nor place to stand
> Would be to me essential,
> If thou and thy white arms were there
> And the fall to doom a long way.

"If war be kind," wrote a clever reviewer, when the second volume appeared, "then Crane's verse may be poetry, Beardsley's black and white creations may be art, and this may be called a book";--a smart summing up that is cher-

ished by cataloguers to this day, in describing the volume
for collectors. Beardsley needs no defenders, and it is
fairly certain that the clever reviewer had not read the book,
for certainly Crane had no illusions about the kindness of
war. The title-poem of the volume is an amazingly beautiful satire which answers all criticism.

> Do not weep, maiden, for war is kind.
> Because your lover threw wild hands toward the sky
> And the affrighted steed ran on alone,
> Do not weep.
> War is kind.
>
> Hoarse, booming drums of the regiment,
> Little souls who thirst for fight,
> These men were born to drill and die.
> The unexplained glory flies above them,
> Great is the battle-god, and his kingdom--
> A field where a thousand corpses lie.
>
>   *   *   *   *
>
> Mother whose heart hung humble as a button
> On the bright splendid shroud of your son,
> Do not weep.
> War is kind.

Poor Stephen Crane! Like most geniuses, he had his
weaknesses and his failings; like many, if not most, geniuses,
he was ill. He died of tuberculosis, tragically young. But
what a comrade he must have been, with his extraordinary
vision, his keen, sardonic comment, his fearlessness and
his failings!

Just a glimpse of Crane's last days is afforded by a
letter written from England by Robert Barr, his friend--
Robert Barr, who collaborated with Crane in "The O' Ruddy,"
a rollicking tale of old Ireland, or, rather, who completed
it at Crane's death, to satisfy his friend's earnest request.
The letter is dated from Hillhead, Woldingham, Surrey, June
8, 1900, and runs as follows:--

My Dear--

    I was delighted to hear from you, and was much
interested to see the article on Stephen Crane you
sent me. It seems to me the harsh judgment of an

unappreciative, commonplace person on a man of genius. Stephen had many qualities which lent themselves to misapprehension, but at the core he was the finest of men, generous to a fault, with something of the old-time recklessness which used to gather in the ancient literary taverns of London. I always fancied that Edgar Allan Poe revisited the earth as Stephen Crane, trying again, succeeding again, failing again, and dying ten years sooner than he did on the other occasion of his stay on earth.

When your letter came I had just returned from Dover, where I stayed four days to see Crane off for the Black Forest. There was a thin thread of hope that he might recover, but to me he looked like a man already dead. When he spoke, or, rather, whispered, there was all the accustomed humor in his sayings. I said to him that I would go over to the Schwarzwald in a few weeks, when he was getting better, and that we would take some convalescent rambles together. As his wife was listening he said faintly: "I'll look forward to that," but he smiled at me, and winked slowly, as much as to say: "You damned humbug, you know I'll take no more rambles in this world." Then, as if the train of thought suggested what was looked on before as the crisis of his illness, he murmured: "Robert, when you come to the hedge--that we must all go over--it isn't bad. You feel sleepy--and--you don't care. Just a little dreamy curiosity--which world you're really in--that's all."

To-morrow, Saturday, the 9th, I go again to Dover to meet his body. He will rest for a little while in England, a country that was always good to him, then to America, and his journey will be ended.

I've got the unfinished manuscript of his last novel here beside me, a rollicking Irish tale, different from anything he ever wrote before. Stephen thought I was the only person who could finish it, and he was too ill for me to refuse. I don't know what to do about the matter, for I never could work up another man's ideas. Even your vivid imagination could hardly conjecture anything more ghastly than the dying man, lying by an open window overlooking the English channel, relating in a sepulchral whisper the comic situations of his humorous hero so that I might take up the thread of his story.

VINCENT STARRETT

From the window beside which I write this I can
see down in the valley Ravensbrook House, where
Crane used to live and where Harold Frederic, he
and I spent many a merry night together.   When the
Romans occupied Britain, some of their legions,
parched with thirst, were wandering about these dry
hills with the chance of finding water or perishing.
They watched the ravens, and so came to the stream
which rises under my place and flows past Stephen's
former home; hence the name, Ravensbrook.

It seems a strange coincidence that the greatest
modern writer on war should set himself down where
the greatest ancient warrior, Caesar, probably stopped
to quench his thirst.

Stephen died at three in the morning, the same
sinister hour which carried away our friend Frederic
nineteen months before.   At midnight, in Crane's
fourteenth-century house in Sussex, we two tried to
lure back the ghost of Frederic into that house of
ghosts, and to our company, thinking that if reappear-
ing were ever possible so strenuous a man as Harold
would somehow shoulder his way past the guards, but
he made no sign.   I wonder if the less insistent
Stephen will suggest some ingenious method by which
the two can pass the barrier.   I can imagine Harold
cursing on the other side, and welcoming the more
subtle assistance of his finely fibred friend.

I feel like the last of the Three Musketeers, the
other two gone down in their duel with Death.   I am
wondering if, within the next two years, I also shall
get the challenge.   If so, I shall go to the competing
ground the more cheerfully that two such good fellows
await the outcome on the other side.

Ever your friend,

Robert Barr.

The last of the Three Musketeers is gone, now, although he outlived his friends by some years.   Robert Barr
died in 1912.   Perhaps they are still debating a joint return.

There could be, perhaps, no better close for a paper
on Stephen Crane than the subjoined paragraph from a letter
written by him to a Rochester editor:--

PRAISE FROM FAMOUS MEN

The one thing that deeply pleases me is the fact that men of sense invariably believe me to be sincere. I know that my work does not amount to a string of dried beans--I always calmly admit it--but I also know that I do the best that is in me without regard to praise or blame. When I was the mark for every humorist in the country, I went ahead; and now when I am the mark for only fifty per cent of the humorists of the country, I go ahead; for I understand that a man is born into the world with his own pair of eyes, and he is not at all responsible for his vision--he is merely responsible for his quality of personal honesty. To keep close to this personal honesty is my supreme ambition.

VINCENT STARRETT.

WALTER PRESCOTT WEBB

"Time does not dim the luster of a good bibliography, but improves it. " So wrote Walter Prescott Webb nearly a quarter of a century ago in an informative introduction to a bibliography of Texas county histories. Perhaps every scholar and user of libraries will grant that bibliographies are important, although most feel no personal obligation to keep them in mind. Even librarians, with few exceptions, have been silent on the service of bibliography to the integrity of research and the culture of the community.

Today, when our tendency to forget simple ways in a desperate preoccupation with computer models (one step removed from reality since man must feed in the data) and other complex ways of doing things, it is reassuring to know that a man of Webb's stature believes that books and bibliography will last indefinitely and that they are a liberating force in society as a whole. His basic conviction, skillfully buttressed by argument and analogy, is this: knowledge matters, not the form it takes. From the beginning books and bibliography are in play as a communications device. Libraries select, organize, and bring the books to the point of use: "They are made available to all and sundry.... The students can now write their themes on county history because they have something to work on. They extend their investigations to the newspaper files, the court records and by interviews.... Some of these young people become writers, and through their work knowledge of the community is further extended. In time comes the novelist to put the story in fiction. The poet puts it in verse and the painter

147

finds that the sunset and the landscape are worthy of
his art. The result is that the life of the community
is affected.... Knowledge spreads about the community, and the people come to feel that they have a
culture and a civilization of their own. "

Texas County Histories: A Bibliography, compiled by H. Bailey Carroll, was published by the
Texas Historical Association in 1943. At the time
he wrote his introduction, Webb was on leave from
the University of Texas to serve as Harmsworth Professor of American History at Oxford (1942-1943).

FOREWORD BY WALTER PRESCOTT WEBB

to H. Bailey Carroll's
Texas County Histories: A Bibliography

I have never believed in the foreword because it always seemed to detract from the dignity of the author and the
intrinsic value of his book. If his book is good, it needs no
introduction; if it is bad, no introduction can add to its merit,
no flattering foreword can lift it up. But my objection does
not apply to this book. This is not really a book. It is a
key to books, a bibliography. Its making does not involve
the ability of the writer as a writer, his competence in style,
or his profundity of ideas. There is no opportunity to talk
about these qualities here.

The first thing I wish to do is to speak of the quality
of the bibliographer. Certainly there can be nothing inspiring
in making a list of books. It is not akin to writing a poem
or a novel. It offers less outlet for the creative instinct
than either biography or documented history. From any
point of view it is painful drudgery and unmitigated toil.
There can be no thrill of joy in the doing and there can be
no material reward. I do not understand bibliographers, but
I do appreciate them because of the service they render and
the hard work they save me and other people. It is of this
service that I can speak.

Bibliographers themselves realize, after it is too late,
the troubles they have involved themselves in. Yet they
seem powerless to escape from the net of their own obses-

sion. Thomas W. Streeter speaks of this in an article which he read before the Bibliographical Society of America: "Many years ago I embarked quite light-heartedly, almost casually, on the project of compiling a critical bibliography of books, broadsides, and maps relating to Texas, 1795-1845.... Raines in his Bibliography of Texas had taken three and a half centuries (1536-1896) for his field. I proposed to limit myself to an interesting half-century ... it appeared to be a comparatively simple task.... What then did this idle task for a winter's evening turn out to be? For the period, Raines cites around 200 titles. For the same period, I have assembled, and am now "agonizing" with, upwards of 1,400. I cite these personal experiences as a warning to the unwary who may feel that destiny has called on them to write the bibliography of some interesting period of a state or region...."

Despite what I have said, the bibliographer often achieves an immortality that is denied to all but a few of his contemporaries. Time does not dim the luster of a good bibliography, but improves it. After the popular novel is forgotten and the "authentic" history is out of date, the bibliography comes into its own. It finds its place on the rare bookshelf, is worn out by use in used libraries, and the perfect copy is exhibited with sadistic joy by the collector who has it to the one who wants it.

The bibliography is a scarce book by the time it is printed because the demand is so limited and the edition is correspondingly small. It soon becomes rare because it is useful. It never gets out of date for the period it covers and with time it becomes more valuable for that period. C. W. Raines' general bibliography of Texas was published, in 1896, at his own expense. This book is today one of the most prized, and most useful, books in any library concerned with Texas, and is indispensable to any collector of Texana. It is quite probable that a good copy of Raines'-- and it needs no further description--would bring more money than he realized in profit for all his labor. The law of compensation eventually gives the bibliographer his reward, post mortem though it may be.

Dr. Carroll has indeed opened a new field in Texas bibliography by listing in one volume the titles of books and articles available on each of the 254 Texas counties. There is little doubt that this key to county histories will make a broader appeal than have most bibliographies. The reasons are not far to seek. The first one is that the book performs a service to 254 local divisions of the state, and no less for the state as a whole. A second reason is found in the convenience of the arrangement: the counties are listed alphabetically and the titles are listed under the counties. It is one thing to have a bibliography on Texas, and quite another to have a bibliography on Bexar, Deaf Smith, or Zavala County. Every editor, teacher, lawyer and minister will find here a key to the historical literature of his own community.

It is only when we come to consider the influence that this book may have on the future that we realize the magnitude of the service here performed. Every intelligent person is, whether he knows it or not, interested in the history of his own family and community or county. When this interest becomes manifest, the first inquiries are: What material is available? Have any books been written? Who wrote them? Who published them? When and where were they published? These inquiries are made at the library, if there be one, at the newspaper office, at the school and of people who buy and read books. The information obtained is in most cases meager. The books themselves are likely to be found only in the few large libraries in the state. The result is that the curiosity of the inquirer about his own community has been baffled and he turns to something else. The presence of one copy of Dr. Carroll's book in the community would answer all the questions raised, or enough of them to encourage further effort.

If there is only one copy, it should be in the best library in the community. When the librarian learns that there is a growing demand for books about the county, she will begin to seek out the books and to buy them. They are made available to all and sundry, and especially to students in the high school. The students can now write their themes on county history because they have something to work on. They extend their investigations to the newspaper files, the court records and by interviews to older citizens who carry valuable memories in their heads. Some of these young people become writers, and through their work knowledge of the community is further extended. In time comes the novelist to put the story in fiction. The poet puts it in verse and the painter finds that the sunset and the landscape are worthy

of his art.   The result is that the life of the whole community is affected.   The people come to know their own
lore.   They prize the oak under which the first court was
held or from which the horsethief hanged.   They take pride
in their own beginnings and see life around them with its
third dimension.   In the meantime the books accumulate in
the community, knowledge spreads about the community, and
the people come to feel that they have a culture and a civilization of their own and not something borrowed or brought in
from a summer trip.   They will love the place, and loving
it, they will take pains to improve it.   Their houses will be
better and their gardens more beautiful.   Native things will
come to be appreciated.   The tree on the hill will cease to
be considered as only so much firewood and the wild flowers
in the pasture as more than so many weeds.   The birds,
solitary wasps and ants are fascinating subjects for study in
every community.   It would be something if each community
in Texas could be such that the youth who leave it will carry
the image of it with them and return to it however far they
may wander.

Some day educators are going to learn something
about education.   I have said that this bibliography is only a
key to books about Texas.   In their turn the books are themselves only keys which admit us into the various rooms of
the mansion of real living.   They are not unlike a microscope, through which we are enabled to see things too small
to be seen unaided, or the telescope, which opens up vistas
of distance otherwise beyond our ken.   The thing that we are
after is not in the microscope or telescope, but at the end
of it, in the focus.   It would seem very silly to gather great
quantities of microscopes and telescopes, place them on
shelves and in catalogues and teach people that education
could be obtained only by a study of these instruments.

Each book has a focus on some aspect of life, and its
purpose is to enable us to see, not the book, but the life at
which the book aims our minds and imaginations.   We shall
never be truly educated until we are able to see things themselves, either through the book or without it.   Let me illus-
trate.   One may know by rote a book about birds, but he can
never know much about birds until he is able to go into the
field, identify them and study for himself their habits and instincts.   The author of the best book might make a mistake
about birds, but the birds themselves make no mistakes

151

where their own actions are concerned. They are the only primary source on birds.

Somehow the notion has got abroad that education is confined to reservations as were the Indians. Books are gathered there and professors aggregate to read or to recommend them. The biggest reservations are called universities and it is too generally assumed that they have a sort of monopoly on knowledge and the facilities for acquiring it. What they really have is a vast number of descriptions which are called books and a somewhat lesser number of describers called teachers. We can never have real education, or a self-perpetuating culture, until we get beyond the description and the describer to the things described. In short, education needs to be got off the reservations, not only for the sake of those who go there for a four year sojourn among the facilities, but for the sake of those who remain in closer contact with the realities.

If books are only descriptions, the only qualification needed to master them is the ability to read; and the requirement for taking in lectures is even less. It is only by looking through the microscope or telescope that we may see things worth while. It is the same with books and professors. We have assembled the mechanism of education in the universities, but fortunately we have not assembled life itself with which true education is solely concerned.

From my point of view, which always seems to me to be a most reasonable one, there is a great hidden university within a radius of five miles of every community. The geology is deeper than any well and the astronomy is firmament high. In between lie all the other branches of knowledge from the mysteries of religious experience to the mathematics of land surveys. The substance of science, art and literature lie about and around us, things too big to be confined on the reservation. We shall have a real culture in Texas when we begin to see that this is so. Then we shall gain the right conception of the function of the university as a place to go to borrow for a time the use of the mechanisms, the descriptions, and all of the facilities with which to extend our vision and enable us to view real things with more understanding and intelligence.

Many years ago it was customary for students who

were finishing college to gather around a bonfire and burn
their books as a token that they were through with the tasks
of learning. The custom of burning books might be revived,
but with an entirely different implication. It should signify
that the individual has discarded the book as he would a crutch
which he no longer needed, and that he is now going forth on
his own intellectual legs to examine the things which the books
called to his attention but revealed so inadequately. Such a
ceremony would indicate that the individual had passed from
the imitative to the creative stage of existence. Education
would then get off the reservation and disperse itself in a
thousand centers over the land.

This bibliography is not going to effect any such revolution as I have hinted at. It is not suggested that there will
be any quick transformation of the cultural pattern. Certainly no Texan, I least of all, would want Texas suddenly converted into Utopia, and thus isolated from the rest of the
world. Perfection is entirely too uniform to suit a land
which approaches perfection closest in its lack of uniformity.
I would not flood the deserts or dry up the swamps; I would
not cover the Panhandle with pine trees or remove them from
the Sabine. I would not change Texas much if I could. She
suits me just as she is, this eternal triangle of forest, desert and plain. What I would do is to encourage study which
would result in a better understanding and a deeper appreciation of Texas. The merit of this bibliography is that it will
contribute to this end.

A word should be said about the authors who have
written the 814 books and articles listed here. For the most
part each has done a labor of love, and in that sense must
be akin to the bibliographer himself. The task of writing
local history, especially in new communities where usually
only scanty records are kept, is prodigious. It requires patience in seeking out material, skill in interviewing and in
harmonizing remembered events with ascertainable facts.
The local historian must exercise nice discrimination between
what he can tell and what can not be told. He often must
close the closest door and pretend that he did not see the
skeleton grinning over the family's past misdeeds.

Since each of these authors was intimately associated
with the life about which he wrote, each has contributed
something to taking education off the reservation. Each

looked closely at local life, found there something worth doing for its own sake, and was the better for doing it. I dare say each history, done at such close range, has taken on in some measure the color, texture and climate of the land described. There must be a suggestion of the fantastic forms and gorgeous lights and shades that forever haunt the memory of him who has seen the counties of the Big Bend and the west. And surely these books from East Texas counties have in them the hue and flavor of red clay, the perfume of the deep forest and the sound of rain on the forest's roof of trees. There must be wind and sun from the plains, but at night wind and sun lie down in quiet together and for a while this vast land is caught in a spell of motionless silence and beauty. Each of these books is like a colored stone, and each of a different color or shade. All of them fitted together form a mosaic of Texas, and since each is in some measure true to its part, the mass is true to the whole. The general historian who can synthesize them and tell the story of Texas with the same fidelity will have written the book that Texas is waiting for. His labor will be arduous, and though this bibliography will ameliorate his labor, it will at the same time increase his responsibility to do the job well. Such a history as I have suggested, built upon the broad foundation of these titles and official sources, might serve to convey some notion of the real life of Texas to those who sojourn on the educational reservations.

It seems that what started out to be a foreword for a bibliography has developed into a theory that true education stems from the earth, from what Hamlin Garland called the verities. Any ultimate effectiveness of education depends upon a recognition of the principle and upon the application of practice to the principle. Each acre of the earth is a library, a museum and a laboratory in which the most marvelous experiments are being carried out. The process of education is simply that of enabling the student to read the books, observe the exhibits, and witness with understanding the experiments. One who can do these things is educated regardless of whether he ever saw the inside of an institution devoted to describing them. It is in this hidden university that we have the substances themselves, the true verities, whereas on the reservations we have only specimens.

This theory is too simple to agree with those unnatural ones which have been taught. It denies that the pro-

cess of education is one of pouring in, as is practiced, or
of drawing out, as is preached. It does not believe that
"the child is the most important factor" and that everything
revolves around him. It denies the validity of pouring, drawing, or revolving as an educational process. The first results in too much fullness, the second in emptiness and the
third in dizziness. It requires no great stretch of the imagination to think of appropriate degrees for each of these
three schools, or to visualize the tripartite procession that
would be certified on graduation as Bachelors of Emptiness,
Masters of Fullness and Doctors of Dizziness.

The name of the theory I propose is the bio-dynamic
theory of education, or a theory of life motion. It implies
a current flowing through a circuit as in electricity. Every
good teacher has had experience with what I am here trying
to describe. It was said that Mark Hopkins could set up
such a circuit by putting himself on one end of a log and a
boy on the other, which simply meant that Mark Hopkins
knew how to handle his apparatus so as to make contact,
start a spark and induce a current of inquiry and learning.

The theory of bio-dynamic agriculture furnishes the
best analogy for educational purposes. The proponents of
that theory hold that the farm is not an inanimate thing, but
a living organism, and that its prosperity depends on setting
up the proper current to keep the organism in good health.
The concept of a farm as a living thing with life currents
throbbing through it is most attractive, so attractive to me
that I bought one. The circuit described for bio-dynamic
agriculture is something like this. The land produces crops,
the crops are fed to the stock, the compost and manure from
the stock, refined by earthworms, are returned to the soil.
By this process a balance is maintained. If any step is neglected disaster results inevitably. The farmer is the technician who keeps the wires in order and the life currents
moving as they should.

Now the purpose of education--I mean real education--
is to set up a current of understanding between the student
and the things of the world in which he lives. In the process
of learning the student begins to look at the things in the
books. We say he studies, and so he does. The only purpose of his study is to get the life current of understanding
started. Once it begins to flicker, he reads more books as

155

his intellectual curiosity drives him on. It is when he is able to lay the book down and examine the rock or the star or the blade of grass for himself and with understanding that he begins to be educated. He still reads books, but only for the short cuts, to gain what advantage he can from the work of others. Once educated, he turns to things not found in universities, but at large.

He must fertilize the anemic hot house plants of knowledge in the compost beds of nature and with the strong, acrid manures of reality before they can grow strong and bear good fruit.

In this bio-dynamic system of education the function of the teacher is plain. He is the farmer, the technician, whose business it is to arrange the apparatus, make the necessary contacts and hope for the spark that sets the mysterious current going. The current flows from the student to the libraries, museums and laboratories, and when a little stronger it takes in the greater life of which these things are but symbols. As the mind expands, the volume increases until it can no longer be confined. It goes out into the world there to be fertilized by the verities. Eventually and inevitably it returns some of its vigor to the field in which it started. Thus is the circuit complete.

This bibliography represents one step in an application of the bio-dynamic principle of education to history. The process seems to have started with the local histories, but each author could probably tell how the spark and the current started in him. Each felt the throb of intellectual excitement between his mind and the things, people, events he was writing about. It will be noted, too, that many of these histories started from low on the ground, from the people of whom they were written. They are very earthy, and in their earthiness they reflect truth.

The next step came when the bibliographer saw the significance of these local accounts and brought them all together in a most useful compendium of reference information. His work has its peculiar value, a unique value, because it rests on a base as broad as the dimensions of Texas and has a substantial point of contact with 254 counties.

Now we must await the historian for whom the way

has been prepared to write the story of Texas, a story which
ought to be true, not only in fact but in spirit and in flavor.
This bibliography will never be far from his reach if he is
to do what is expected. Such a book, when it comes, will
complete the circuit and contribute in a thousand communities
to a richer culture risen from the fertile soil of humble local
histories.

                              WALTER PRESCOTT WEBB
The Queen's College
Oxford
November 11, 1942

One night in London, in November, 1933, James
Hilton dreamed up Good-Bye, Mr. Chips. Within a
week the entire story was finished. Reprinted fifteen times in the first six months, in ever larger
editions, it proved a difficult book to keep in stock.
Hilton said himself that it was "written and first
printed in its native land, ... discovered by America,
and later came back to England with the success that
America had given it." While it is hardly possible
to discover an author who had already written and
published some twelve books, American critics may
take credit for having reached down a helping hand
to give Mr. Chips a rousing send-off in this country. Praise poured in from everywhere. In his
short but illuminating introduction to Good-Bye, Mr.
Chips, Edward Weeks, then serving as an assistant
to the editor of the Atlantic Monthly, wrote "everywhere you went you heard people talking about Mr.
Chips as if he were someone they had known."

The "who's who" facts on James Hilton are that
he was born in Lancashire in 1900 and taken to live
in London at an early age, where he attended various schools. His father, a schoolmaster, is me-
morialized in Mr. Chips. James entered Cambridge
with a scholarship and graduated with honors. In
1937 he took up residence in California. Many
Americans remember him as the inventor of that
mythical land of eternal youth he called Shangri-la.
During World War II the term became widely known
as the supposed base of an American raid on Japan
when President Roosevelt facetiously announced that
the bombers had taken off from Shangri-la.

Good-Bye, Mr. Chips has no plot--only inci-

cents recollected in retirement by the classics master, Arthur Chipping, who taught at a boys' school
which the author describes as "a good public school
of the second rank." A bachelor, quiet, conservative, one who did not hold with the modern newness
of Bernard Shaw, Ibsen, and women bicycling, he
was regarded by his fellow teachers and successive
generations of students as a "decent fellow and a
hard worker" but somewhat dry and a bit of a drone.
But then at the age of 48 he met young Katherine
Bridges, fell in love with her blue flashing eyes and
freckled cheeks, and married her. This momentous
event transformed him into the salty and lovable
character that made him a legend among school-
masters.

There one has the core of the story. It is really only a novelette which takes about an hour or two
to read but the memory of Mr. Chips lingers on.
That is the reason why, of course, as Mr. Weeks
notes in his introduction, people wrote the author
from all parts of the globe "to say that they had been
taught by the original Mr. Chips."

FOREWORD BY EDWARD WEEKS

to James Hilton's
Good-bye, Mr. Chips

James Hilton was not only a very good novelist, he
was a very good talker. Though he was English-born, he
lived for the latter part of his life in California, and on my
visits to the Coast I always looked forward to having a leisurely dinner with him, in the course of which we would
compare notes about everything under the sun. I remember
well our last meeting, for it occurred shortly after we had
learned for sure that the Russians had perfected, far ahead
of schedule, their atomic bomb. Jimmie was depressed by
the news, for in his farsighted way he saw at once that this
would involve us in the most dangerous armament race in
human history.

I knew that he was at work on a new novel and at a
favorable opening I asked how it was going. "I have made

four beginnings, " he said. "I think I have got a good idea
and for about a week I'll start off each morning at the type-
writer with a feeling of confidence. And then just after I
have passed page fifty, it is as if the words 'So what!' suddenly stood out in capitals on the page. We haven't got the
confidence we once had, now that we know about those bombs.
It is a hard time in which to try to write fiction."

Good-bye, Mr. Chips, Hilton's most successful novel,
and surely the most endearing portrait of a schoolteacher in
our time, was written in another kind of desperation. In
November, 1933, James Hilton was struggling to meet his
deadline for a story for the Christmas issue of the British
Weekly. He needed the fifty pounds (then two hundred and
fifty dollars) he would be paid for the story; and he hadn't
an idea. After a sleepless night, he rose and went for a
bicycle ride in the foggy dawn. When he returned, ravenous,
for breakfast he had his lead, and Mr. Chips was written in
longhand and almost without alteration in the four days that
followed. It was published with little notice in London, but
when it appeared in the Atlantic the following April, the
American acclaim woke up the English. Everywhere you
went you heard people talking about Mr. Chips as if he were
someone they had known. Bishop William A. Lawrence spoke
of Mr. Chips in a sermon at Trinity Church in Boston; William Lyon Phelps, the most quoted professor in New Haven,
said it was "a masterpiece and ought to be so regarded a
hundred years from now"; and Alexander Woollcott, who as
the Town Crier had a more stimulating effect on readers at
that period than any other single person, devoted a whole
broadcast to Mr. Chips, which he called "the most profoundly
moving story that has passed this way in several years."

To Jimmie Hilton the theme was as natural as breath-
ing. His father was a headmaster, and at the boarding
school where Jimmie was sent, he was happy. Had he cared
more for athletics he might have been less observant of his
teachers. But he was a roly-poly, good tempered, and no
good at games. His mind was inquiring and responsive: he
wrote poems about the Russian Revolution and the sinking of
the Lusitania, and broke all speed records for reciting the
long Latin grace.

Mr. Chips, as Hilton drew him, is a composite; he
has the wise and sweetening influence of Jimmie's father, the

160

discipline and idiosyncrasy of his Latin teacher, and the unsparing devotion which the profession demands of all. And this was why people wrote him from all parts of the globe to say that they had been taught by the original Mr. Chips. He was thirty-three when he wrote this story, but it established him for life.

EDWARD WEEKS

EUDORA WELTY

It is asserted that out of several hundred mysteries published each year, about a dozen are so far superior to the rest they they repay re-reading. In her anthology, entitled <u>Hanging by a Thread,</u> Miss Joan Kahn confines herself to thirty-six which make the grade and which range in time from Tacitus's "The Death of Agrippina, The Mother of Nero" to Dashiell Hammett's "The Scorched Face." They are absolutely first rate, a rare combination, some imaginary and others historical, providing a well-drawn cast of authors and characters, not limited by time or place but strictly by high literary quality.

Eudora Welty, whose own tales of naïve-sophisticated fantasy often show a weakness for improbable and melodramatic situations, is here appropriately in the role of introducer. Not parsimonius in her praise, she compares the anthology to an Easter egg hunt in which "I consider every egg in her basket a good find, a bright choice, and the whole a feast to sit down to." Among her profiles of the authors which are her special favorites in the collection are William Roughead, the chronicler of famous Scottish trials; Edmund Pearson, librarian and bibliophile; Joseph Henry Jackson, former literary editor of the <u>San Francisco Chronicle</u>; Edmund Knox, long associated in various literary capacities with the British humor magazine, <u>Punch</u>; and Montague R. James, mediaeval scholar and former provost at Eton.

Much of the pleasure of reading detective and mystery stories is the just release from the boredom and monotony of everyday facts. They divert because they tell of experiences outside the ordinary. Eudora

Welty shrewdly comments in her introduction on the
art of creating the kind of suspense which will be-
guile the literate reader, tax his wits, amuse him,
or arouse his moral judgments. Her own robust
humor is revealed in her sketch of the Joseph Henry Jackson story, "Other Than a Good One," one
of her favorites in Miss Kahn's anthology. For example, there is the "impulsive Emma LeDoux, who
got rid of her husband, all right--she gave him
knock-out drops of morphine and packed him in a
trunk; and had him carted off to the baggage room
of the Southern Railway station in Stockton--she just
forgot to consign him to anybody." "The gravest
mistakes in crime," she comments, "are so often
matters of domestic routine or of common politeness."

INTRODUCTION BY EUDORA WELTY

to Joan Kahn's
Hanging by a Thread

     Joan Kahn, the editor to whose discoveries we owe
some of the best and liveliest suspense fiction being published
today, has given us here another discerning and highly individual collection.

     The editor of an anthology is normally commended by
the writer of its Introduction in proportion to how far out of
his way he has traveled in collecting the Table of Contents.
Anthology editing is treated like an Easter Egg hunt. But I
am a much older reader than I am an Introduction writer,
and I know the reader sits waiting in hope for the Golden
Egg, rather than for some colorless fossil, however long it
has been lying under the hedge being missed by all the other
editors. Miss Kahn has indeed ranged far and with a fine
freedom, and she deserves credit for resourcefulness. But
I would have expected it of her, and this Introduction gives
her highest credit for what she has come up with. I would
consider every egg in her basket a good find, a bright
choice, and the whole a feast to sit down to.

     Among the thirty-six selections--that's a generous

number--are some that are familiar, in the comforting sense
of the word; we look to see if our dearest love is here, and
he is--and others that are likely to be quite new to most
readers.   Stories, essays, and historical accounts have been
chosen from both here and abroad, from over no narrow
stretch of time.   (There's one that comes out of Latin writings of the first century.)   They range from tragedy (Camus)
to parody (E. V. Knox) and include Dashiell Hammett, Dylan
Thomas, Lord Dunsany, and Thurber.   Suspense, as the title
tells us, is the common factor.   But it is not the measure,
really.

Suspense, per se, is of not too much account.   Painful, pleasurable, or no opinion, suspense by itself is to a
reader sensation only.   It has one positive quality, duration.
And, by itself, murder is not the criterion for excellence.
The reader who reads for the sake of the crime itself--he
exists, because look what's in the bookstore--is the first
victim of the blunt instrument of its usual prose style.   He
has never been beguiled; he has never been brought to astonishment at the human race; he has never had his wits or
his moral judgment or his amusement aroused; he has hardly
had any suspense, for he has got what was coming to him
very early, perhaps on page one.

Indeed murder is brutal.   But there is a wonder to
the human act which can only be approached through the
mind, for it lies in the mind--in the mind of the murderer
or that of his victim or possibly, more often than we know,
in the peculiar combination of the two minds meeting.   Murder's fascination for the reader stems from wonder, and has
nothing to do with what De Quincey in scorn expressed as "a
knife, a purse, and a dark lane."   The fascination of Joan
Kahn's Hanging by a Thread is the thread itself--that thread
of human frailty on which, so often and so literally, life and
death depend.

I should say that what the present authors all have in
common is a civilized intellect and a distinction of charm or
brilliance or beauty about their writing, all of which concerns, to use William Roughead's word, "the criminous."

It is this essayist, with a wisdom so becoming to his
prose, the affection he feels for his poor, wayward fools of
fellow beings so contagious to his reader, who for many

more than myself, I feel, will constitute the Golden Egg here. He is well represented in "The Sandyford Mystery. " As always, he examines the case on trial with the carefullest appreciation for the unpredictable, the eccentric, the sublimely impulsive, the staunchly wicked, the staggeringly optimistic souls he finds so "attaching. " In Roughead terms, the deeds brought to light in the courtroom in Glasgow are "unseemly" or "regrettable"; three footprints are "considerately left intact by the criminal when washing the rest of the bedroom floor"; he is forced to remark on the "inconsiderate persistence" of the counsel for the defense of poor, innocent Jess M'Pherson. Roughead observed a self-imposed limitation of his writings to cases in his native Scotland, and they gave him gracious scope for his work; but occasionally he did cast a fond look across the water at our own Lizzie Borden. She was after his heart--he called her "unfilial. "

Lizzie Borden, of course, was the property of Edmund Pearson. He was of the Roughead persuasion and was, like him, a writer of great charm. Like him too, Pearson was a learned man; he was a librarian and bibliophile who had had experience on the Federal Grand Jury. In order to discuss "that elusive creature, Jack the Ripper, " without plunging into melodrama, it was necessary to turn over a ton of rubbish and, in addition, to read half a shelf-full of reliable books, " he said in the preface to one of his books. "What the vulgar never understand, but what the erudite know perfectly, is that many murders are trumpery affairs, worth a paragraph in a newspaper, and then oblivion. Perhaps only two or three times a year, throughout the whole round world, may be discovered an almost flawless gem, meriting the attention of Thomas De Quincey himself. " In his "Miss Holland's Elopement" which Miss Kahn gives us, he typically produces a sample of the correspondence that Mr. S. Herbert Dougal carries on from his cell (he is suspected, quite correctly, of putting poor Miss Holland of Moat Farm in the moat) with the many ladies of his acquaintance: "I dare say the girls have received their notices to attend next Monday ... have they not? [He refers to the trial.] There will be several from about there, and it would be a good idea to club together and hire a trap and drive all the way. It is a delightful drive through undulating country, and ... would be a veritable treat for them all. "

Of this same brotherhood was the engaging Joseph

Henry Jackson. Of his pieces on murder in the western branch, "'Other Than a Good One'" is a good one: impulsive Emma LeDoux, who got rid of her husband, all right--she gave him knock-out drops and morphine and packed him in a trunk; and had him carted off to the baggage room of the Southern Pacific railway station there in Stockton--she just forgot to consign him to anybody. On the other hand, the above Jess, in sending a box of bloodstained clothing off for the murderer--as she knew him to be, but in the confusion of her terror she was doing him the favor--dispatched it to "apocryphal consignees" and that helped to put her in the dock instead of him. The gravest mistakes in crime are so often matters of domestic routine or of common politeness.

The collection gives us an opportunity to observe another thing about ourselves: we feel differently about criminals according to the time we live in. Russel Crouse's account of the murder of Arnold Rothstein, for instance, succeeds in setting the Twenties much farther back from us than the years account for. Gangsters take on a sort of unearthly quality of simple, self-seeking adventure, such as was once attributed to the financial wizards. (This is not through a flaw in Mr. Crouse's reporting; it emerges from the feeling of the times.) They said it with bullets--a style of romantic self-delusion and self-glorification different from ours today, which tends to be more introspective, as there will be some other style to follow ours. There are fashions in crime and in punishment, as we must observe, and, alas, in justice itself. In his studies of human frailty Roughead never exempted the jury, but gave them equal prominence with the prisoner in the box; and, as is well known, after the unjust and absurd conviction of Oscar Slater, whose trial he covered in the "British Trials" volume, he bent his own efforts for years on Slater's behalf, until the man was freed.

Indeed, distance in time is an unreliable gauge by which to tell what can be real and what can't be. Take the eighteenth-century account of Latude's set forth here. That trunk! Out of his trunk--for it has accompanied him to the Bastille where he is confined without hope of pardon--this prisoner takes "twelve dozens of shirts" and, as needed, "napkins, nightcaps, stockings, drawers, pocket handkerchiefs--everything which could supply thread or silk"--and unravels every thread and twists it all into fourteen hundred

feet of assorted ropes--all in secret, of course--and gets
himself and his fellow prisoner up the chimney and down the
tower and through the moat to safety.   It is a terrible account, one of incredible bravery and ingenuity and persistence,
and yet it reads like a fairy tale.   This is the fault simply
and solely of the trunk.   While fiction must carry the ring
of truth, the actuality is seldom safe from sounding like fantasy.

But time--and it is the longest time in the book--has
not been able to affect Tacitus.   Read the story of Nero getting his mother murdered.   That wasn't easy, either, for his
mother knew even sooner than Nero did that he would murder
her--it had been foretold at his birth; but they were in mutual
suspense over how it would be brought about and how soon.
The account is hair-raisingly real; it is most powerfully
strange and there is nowhere a trace of fantasy.

The articles are a hard measure for the stories to
come up to, but Miss Kahn has chosen equally widely and
well, it seems to this reader.   Dashiell Hammett, who wrote
with delicacy and in a fadeless kind of acid, is here appropriately to lead off the book.   The editor, quick to discover
the new, has also made discoveries of the old in hitherto un-
detected places: in Harper's New Monthly Magazine of October, 1858, is a story by Mr. Wilkie Collins called "A Marriage Tragedy," and you may read it here.   She has found
some good odd ones, like Robert Borger's "The Other Place."
There are some masterpieces.   "A Strange Murderer" from
Gorky's Fragments from My Diary plumbs the whole deep of
murder when the murderer speaks of the thing he has learned
from his crime, the secret: it is the vulnerability of all
mankind.   "'Everybody was afraid of me and I was afraid of
everybody.'"

And there is the ghost story, which the Victorians
certainly did better than anybody else.   Even the lesser
thriller of that period can retain its freezing powers after
you might uncharitably think it has dried up, as a dead bee
can still sting you if you touch it.   "My curiosity is not satisfied," says a character who has just spent the required night
in a haunted house, "but it is quenched."   That is Bulwer-
Lytton.

I am partial myself to the author of "Lost Hearts."

PRAISE FROM FAMOUS MEN

Here is the little boy arriving, as the clock in the church tower is striking six of an evening in early autumn, at the house of his elderly cousin of whose "pursuits and temper" very little is known but whose library is known to contain "all the then available books bearing on the Mysteries, the Orphic poems, the worship of Mithras, and the Neo-Platonists"--M. R. James, of course: who else knew that villains were recognizable by their libraries?

I was glad as well to see "The Sea Raiders" here, for the tight and expert hold that H. G. Wells in his tales can exert upon a reader's worst fears is not often enough praised or highly enough estimated, to my mind. "For a time nothing but eyes, and then ... tentacles streaming out and parting the weed fronds this way and that. "

Where Joan Kahn shows her editorial hand most distinctively is made known, it seems to me, by the remaining thing that the contributors have in common. All the voices are gentle. The voice of understanding does not need to be raised. In this collection, we may hear in turn the voice of the scholar, of the jurist, of the teller of tales, of the historian, the romancer, and the pure entertainer; but all of them are the voices of those whose hope it is to give pleasure. They are very welcome to the ear.

EDMUND WILSON

Ernest Hemingway was born two years before the turn of the century and died by suicide sixty-three years later in his home in Ketchum, Idaho. His wife, Mary, heard the shotgun explosion and found the body of the bearded writer sprawled on the floor of the foyer in a pool of blood. The savagery of his death was reminiscent of the executions and wartime atrocities which he interpolated between the short stories of his book, In Our Time (1925). Credit goes to Edmund Wilson, who provides a preface to the book, for being the first to perceive what was great in Hemingway. In the Dial for October 1924, he pointed out that "Hemingway's poems are not particularly important but his prose is of the first distinction."

In Our Time is an extraordinary mixture. It consists of vignettes of war, in which violence bursts forth nakedly, sandwiched between short stories about a boy named Nick who grew up in the Michigan backwoods. Wilson perceives in these contrasting elements of brutality and sensitivity the dramatic counterpart which characterizes all of Hemingway's writings. The range of the conflicts may be gauged by the story of the boy's father, a physician, performing a Caesarian operation on an Indian's squaw with a jack-knife while the Indian, who cannot bear it, slits his throat in his bunk; the soldier boy who waited for the German to get one leg over the garden wall and then "potted him," and the same boy, shot in the spine and dying, deciding in his death agony that "he will make a separate peace"; and the brutal brakeman who, pretending friendliness with Nick, knocks him off a freight car, and the

169

formal courtesy of Bugs, the Negro, who feeds him
around the campfire. As Edmund Wilson points out,
"Life is fine: the woods are enjoyable; being with
one's friends is enjoyable; even the War is enjoyable. But the brutality of life is always there, and
it is somehow bound up with the enjoyment."

In his austere, crisp style, Hemingway evokes
the countryside, creating not a background but an
ambience. You feel and taste the smoke and Irish
whiskey while two youths carry on an endless and
aimless conversation before an open fire; you shiver
in the icy blast which comes off the big lake; you
actually see the trout lying on the pebbles in a clear
stream. Hemingway was fascinated by the outdoors,
fishing, hunting, conversation, and drinking. He
loved all sports, including bull-fighting, of course,
which is violent and cruel, but not cruel sport, because it is no sport at all.

INTRODUCTION BY EDMUND WILSON

to Ernest Hemingway's
In Our Time: Stories

"In Our Time" is Ernest Hemingway's first book,
and it has the appearance of a miscellany. It consists of sketches and short stories, among which we
are able to recognize, as we reread them, early experiments with almost all the themes which he has since treated
more elaborately. There are bull-fight scenes; drinking
conversations; Gertrude Stein comedy; memories of the Italian front. And one piece, "A Very Short Story," is a sort
of scenario for "A Farewell to Arms," with an ending perhaps more convincing than the rather romanticized idyll of
the novel.

Yet "In Our Time" is complete and satisfactory in itself: it has the whole of Hemingway in it already. And its
very mixed and fragmentary character enables us to understand this whole, to identify its various elements, better than
any of his subsequent books has done. "In Our Time" is
made up of two alternating series: a set of short stories
dealing chiefly with the growing-up of a boy in the American

Northwest; and sandwiched in with these, a set of brief and brutal sketches of happenings mostly connected with the War. The sensitiveness and candor of the boy strike a sharp discord with the cold-bloodedness and barbarity of the executions, the police shootings and the battles; but though the boy appears in one of the intermediary sketches as a wounded soldier, hit in the spine and ready to "make a separate peace," it does not require this to establish a relation between the two series. They both represent the same world, and the contrast which at first disconcerts us is at the centre of Hemingway's point of view. It is the source of the peculiar emotional effects which his later books have been able to produce so powerfully.

Candor and cold-bloodedness both belong to the same humanity. Has the young man who gets wounded in the War, who watches the cabinet ministers shot and who pots the enemy as they are trying to get over a simply priceless barricade, really come such a long way from the boy who went fishing at Big Two-Hearted River? Was not life back in the Michigan woods equally destructive and cruel? In an Indian shanty, a squaw had once had to have a Caesarian operation with a jack-knife and without anaesthetic, and the Indian hadn't been able to bear it and had cut his throat in his bunk; Nick's father, who is a doctor, had saved the life of another squaw, and the Indian had insolently picked a quarrel with him rather than pay him with work; Nick himself had sent his girl about her business when he had found out how terrible her mother was. Life is fine: the woods are enjoyable; fishing is enjoyable; being with one's friends is enjoyable; even the War is enjoyable. But the brutality of life is always there, and it is somehow bound up with the enjoyment. Bull-fights are especially enjoyable. Even Nick's fishing-trip, when he is away by himself happy and free in the woods, has aspects which must make it unique among the fishing-trips of literature--for through all Nick's tranquil exhilaration we are made conscious in a curious way of the cruelty involved for the fish--and not only this, but even of the martyrdom of the grasshoppers used for bait. The condition of life is still pain--and every calm or contented surface still vibrates with its pangs. The resolution of that discord in art makes the beauty of Hemingway's stories.

"In Our Time" thus provides a sort of key to Heming-

171

way's later and more ambitious books. Suffering and making
suffer, and their relation to the sensual enjoyment of life,
are the subject of them all--though the evenness, the prose
perfection, of the surface in these books seems sometimes
to have concealed from their readers the conflicts which it
covers but which it has been stretched so taut precisely to
convey. "A Farewell to Arms," which probably contains
Hemingway's best narrative and most moving scenes, seems
to me in some ways less characteristic and less interesting
in this respect than "The Sun Also Rises" and his short stories; because in "A Farewell to Arms" the making suffer is
all blamed on things in general, and the hero and heroine
are represented as perfectly innocent victims with no relation to the forces that torment them: their story lacks the
conflict of impulses which makes the real drama in Hemingway, and when they emerge from the stream of action, when
they escape together after the Caporetto retreat, we cease
to believe in them as human personalities. "The Sun Also
Rises," on the other hand, has a profound unity and a disquieting reality because there is an intimate relation established between the fiesta in the little Spanish town, with its
processions, its bull-fighting and its hilarity, and the atro-
cious behavior of the group of Americans and English who
have come down from Paris to enjoy it. In the heartlessness
of these people toward each other we recognize the same
principle at work as in the pagan orgy of the festival. The
persecution of Cohn is as much a natural casualty of a bar-
barous world as the unexpected fate of the man who gets ac-
cidentally gored by the bull on the way to the bull-ring.
Hemingway's most remarkable effects in this book are those,
as in the fishing-trip, where we are made to feel behind the
gusto of the appetite for the physical world the falsity or the
tragedy of a moral situation. This undruggable consciousness of something wrong seems never to arouse Hemingway
to passionate violence; but it poisons him and makes him
sick, and this invests with a singular sinister quality--a
quality I suppose new in fiction--the sunlight and the green
summer landscapes of "The Sun Also Rises."

The interest of "The Sun Also Rises" arises from the
attempts of the hero and heroine to disengage themselves
from such a world, or rather to find some way of living in
it honorably. Life, which we devour so voraciously for the
very things about it which destroy us, is always in the long
run a losing game; but it is a game and at least allows of

172

the kind of virtues proper to a game. We must stick to the
code of the sportsman and lose in a sportsmanlike way. And
so the bull-fight itself, with which Hemingway has always
been so much preoccupied, becomes a symbol of life: you
stab or you get gored--and in the meantime many unoffending
horses are casually being disembowelled; the highest aim is
to kill the bull, or if the time has come to die, to die game
--like the old bull-fighter in "The Undefeated." This con-
ceiving of life as a game--even though Hemingway's favorite
sport is bull-fighting--is peculiarly Anglo-Saxon. How Anglo-
Saxon it is we realize when we think of Maupassant or Dostoevsky, both occupied like Hemingway with the problem of
suffering and making suffer, and when we see how completely
different are the terms in which this problem presents itself
to them. And though Hemingway can hardly yet be compared
to Dostoevsky, he is certainly, I should say, a more interesting writer than Maupassant. When we put them together,
we recognize how much is conventional and mechanical in
Maupassant's French pessimism, and we feel, on the other
hand, that Hemingway has invested the Anglo-Saxon idea of
sport with a seriousness which not even Kipling had previously been able to give it.

At any rate, Hemingway's artistic personality has already come of age in "In Our Time." It is the book, not of
an amateur, but of an artist who has already found his voca-
tion--who, though he is still trying out with small subjects,
displays already a mastery of his craft. The naive col-
loquial accent--partly learned from Sherwood Anderson and
Gertrude Stein--is already a limpid shaft in deep waters.
The bull-fight sketches have the dry sharpness and elegance
of Goya's lithographs. Yet Hemingway should perhaps more
than any one else be allowed to escape the common literary
fate of being derived from other people. He is one of the
most original of contemporary writers. There have been
few first-rate writers in the United States, but these, if they
have been often peculiarly isolated, have been also likely to
be peculiarly original. They have created for themselves
directly new and personal ways of writing for personal ways
of seeing and feeling. And with the descriptions in "In Our
Time" of American wood and water Hemingway has brought
into literature a new pair of eyes for landscape, as in his
sketches of the War, where the steady cheerful tone of everyday wakes such strange qualms of insecurity and anguish, he
catches as they have never yet been caught the blind excited

emotions of the American of 1917 and thereafter.

EDMUND WILSON.

LEONARD WOOLF

   The name Bloomsbury is so often linked with
Virginia Woolf, British born novelist and essayist,
that it may be well to say a word about it for the
benefit of readers who were born since World War
II. The so-called Bloomsbury Group, a fascinating
and somewhat bizarre group of eccentrics, made its
first appearance about 1910, exercised its greatest
influence in the twenties, and came to an end with
the death of Virginia Woolf. The name is associated with a residential area in metropolitan West
London centered around the British Museum and
including such well-known squares as Russell, Bed-
ford and Bloomsbury. Most of its members were
graduates of Cambridge and came from cultured,
well-off families. They included writers, artists,
musicians and others who rebelled against the conventions of Victorian society and stood for "the importance of human relations and for personal integrity." Virginia and her husband, Leonard Woolf,
were prominent members of the Group. In 1917
they founded their own private press, the Hogarth
Press, which was used for printing their books and
those of their friends.
   Thirty-five years after her death by suicide in
1941, Virginia Woolf is still very much alive. Indeed, one of the editors of her recently published
letters--the first of a projected six-volume set--
claims that she "will be read and written about for
centuries to come." Selections from her diary, entitled A Writer's Diary, were published by her husband in 1953, followed by a biography by her nephew
Quentin Bell. Without doubt the major new work is
the letters mentioned above; it has been announced

that the complete text of her twenty-six volumes of
diary is now in preparation under the editorship of
Olivier Bell.

Virginia Woolf's genius--for she was a kind of
genius--is more apparent to the general reader in
her concise and straightforward A Writer's Diary
than in her experimental novels, which are rather
incoherent, have no obvious form, and which quite
frankly bore most readers even though they are
widely applauded by higher thinkers. There is a
touch of bitchiness about her comments on friends
and enemies. She opens the diary with an explosive attack on Christina Rossetti: "First she
starved herself of love, which meant also life; then
of poetry in deference to what she thought her religion demanded." Of her friend, the popular novelist Katherine Mansfield, she writes: "her mind
is very thin soil, laid an inch or two deep upon
very barren rock ... She is content with superficial smartness." Of her friend and enemy Arnold
Bennett, whom she encounters at a party allegedly
engineered by himself to "get on good terms with
Mrs. Woolf," she writes: "He at last articulates
quietly ... but the method lengthens out intolerably
a rather uninspired discourse. I like the old creature. I do my best, as a writer, to detect signs of
genius in his smoky brown eye." She attends a
week-end party at Garsington and speaks of "the
slipperiness" of Lady Ottoline's soul (a wealthy
hostess, whose country estate afforded something of
a haven for pacifists and the pacifist intelligentsia
during World War I), and of Mrs. Asquith, "stone
white; with the brown veiled eyes of an aged fal-
con." Her literary judgments are not all severe by
any means. Byron was "full of ideas--a quality that
gives his verse a toughness." Of Paradise Lost she
writes: "I get no help in judging life; I scarcely
feel that Milton lived or knew men and women ...
but how smooth, strong and elaborate it all is.
What poetry! I can conceive that even Shakespeare
after this would seem a little troubled, personal,
hot, and imperfect."

Such bald, uncompromising judgments are to
be found only in a diary, of course, but there are
entries which show a much warmer side to Virginia

Woolf. She frequently shows herself affectionate and
deeply sympathetic with the misfortune of others.
Taking an old lady a gift of plums and hearing her
repeat over and over again her miseries and suffer-
ings, she records "Human ingenuity in torture is very
great." When visiting a fellow writer, Francis Bir-
rell, lying in a hotel bedroom fearful that he "may
die under another operation, or slowly stiffen into
complete paralysis," she tries to calm his fears,
kisses him twice, and then leaves quickly so that
he would not see her tears. It is perhaps surprising to find that this childless woman is very fond of
children; "There's a quality in their minds to me
adorable; to be alone with them, and see them day
to day would be an extraordinary experience." It is
even more unexpected to discover the practical and
mundane in such a highly imaginative and unrealistic
person, as when she tabulates her possible sales and
schemes for a new bathroom, "I'm out to make £300
this summer by writing and build a bath and hot water range at Rodmell."

In his introduction to his wife's diary, Leonard
Woolf says that he tried to include three types of
material: extracts where the diary was used as a
kind of trial run for her published writings; passages
which show the impact upon her mind of persons and
places; and comment on books. Considering the
prominence of Virginia Woolf's family and the circles in which she and her husband moved, persons
do not occupy her attention as much as one might
expect in the selections published in the expurgated
diary. Perhaps one reason was that she felt terribly frustrated when too many interruptions slowed
down the flow of her ideas and writing. The diary,
as most diaries are, is obviously self-revealing, but
her husband in his introduction warns the reader not
to take this fragment of the full diary as a self-portrait. Nevertheless, the great value of the diary re-
sides in telling truthfully and frankly the story of
what a writer's life is like in its day-to-day routine,
what its worries are, and what its rewards are. It
is especially important in Virginia Woolf's life because the diary covered the period during which her
three finest books, To the Lighthouse, Waves, and
Between the Acts were written and published. It

begins with the ending of one great war and closes
with the beginning of another. It is a narrative of
frustrations and feelings of emptiness and pointless-
ness, but also one of achievement.

PREFACE BY LEONARD WOOLF

to Virginia Woolf's
A Writer's Diary

In 1915 Virginia Woolf began regularly to write a diary. She continued to do so until 1941 and the last entry
is four days before her death. She did not write it regularly
every day. There are sometimes entries daily for several
days; more usually there is an entry every few days and
then there will perhaps be a gap of a week or two. But the
diary gives for 27 years a consecutive record of what she
did, of the people whom she saw, and particularly of what
she thought about those people, about herself, about life,
and about the books she was writing or hoped to write. She
wrote it on blank sheets of paper (8 1/4" by 10 1/2", i.e.
technically large post quarto). At first the sheets were
clipped together with loose-leaf rings, but all the later diaries are in bound volumes. We used to have the sheets
bound up in paper over boards, and the cover paper is nearly always one of the coloured, patterned Italian papers which
we frequently used for binding books of poetry published by
us in The Hogarth Press and of which she was very fond.
We used to buy the paper for the sheets and have it bound
up in books ready for her to use, and she wrote her novels
in this kind of book as well as her diary. When she died,
she left 26 volumes of diary written in this kind of book in
her own hand.

The diary is too personal to be published as a whole
during the lifetime of many people referred to in it. It is,
I think, nearly always a mistake to publish extracts from
diaries or letters, particularly if the omissions have to be
made in order to protect the feelings or reputations of the
living. The omissions almost always distort or conceal the
true character of the diarist or letter-writer and produce
spiritually what an Academy picture does materially, smooth-
ing out the wrinkles, warts, frowns, and asperities. At the

best and even unexpurgated, diaries give a distorted or one-
sided portrait of the writer, because, as Virginia Woolf herself remarks somewhere in these diaries, one gets into the
habit of recording one particular kind of mood--irritation or
misery, say--and of not writing one's dairy when one is feeling the opposite. The portrait is therefore from the start un-
balanced, and, if someone then deliberately removes another
characteristic, it may well become a mere caricature.

Nevertheless the present book is composed of extracts
from Virginia Woolf's diaries. She used her diary partly, in
the normal way of diarists, to record what she did and what
she thought about people, life, and the universe. But she
also used it in a very individual way as a writer and artist.
In it she communed with herself about the books she was
writing or about future books which she intended to write.
She discusses the day-to-day problems of plot or form, of
character or exposition, which she encounters in each of her
books as she conceives them or writes or revises them.
Her position as an artist and the merits of her books are a
subject of dispute, and no prudent man would claim to judge
to a nicety the place which a contemporary writer will occupy
in the pantheon of letters. Some critics are irritated and
many less sophisticated readers are bewildered by her later
novels. But no one denies that she was a serious artist and
there are many people who, like Professor Bernard Blackstone, have no doubt that "she was a great artist," that "she
did supremely well what no one else has attempted to do,"
and that her "world will survive as the crystal survives under the crushing rock-masses" [Virginia Woolf, by Bernard
Blackstone, pp36, 37, 38 (British Council & Longmans,
Green, London, 1952)]. And it is relevant to what I have
to say in this preface that many of the people who cannot
understand or dislike or ridicule her novels agree that in
The Common Reader and her other books of essays she showed
herself to be a very remarkable literary critic.

I have been carefully through the 26 volumes of diary
and have extracted and now publish in this volume practically
everything which referred to her own writing. I have included also three other kinds of extract. The first consists
of a certain number of passages in which she is obviously
using the diary as a method of practising or trying out the
art of writing. The second consists of a few passages which,
though not directly or indirectly concerned with her writings,

PRAISE FROM FAMOUS MEN

I have deliberately selected because they give the reader an idea of the direct impact upon her mind of scenes and persons, i. e. of the raw material of her art. Thirdly I have included a certain number of passages in which she comments upon the books she was reading.

The book throws light upon Virginia Woolf's intentions, objects, and methods as a writer. It gives an unusual psychological picture of artistic production from within. Its value and interest naturally depend to a great extent upon the value and interest of the product of Virginia Woolf's art. Unless I had agreed with Professor Blackstone, I would not have edited and published this book. She was, I think, a serious artist and all her books are serious works of art. The diaries at least show the extraordinary energy, persistence, and concentration with which she devoted herself to the art of writing and the undeviating conscientiousness with which she wrote and rewrote and again rewrote her books. The Waves seems to me a great work of art, far and away the greatest of her books. To the Lighthouse and Between the Acts should also, I think, live in their own right, while the other books, though on a lower level of achievement, are, as I said, "serious" and will always be worth reading and studying. I put forward this opinion, not as of any value, but as an explanation of my publishing the book.

In editing the diary I was in some doubt whether to indicate omissions. In the end I decided not to do so as a general rule. The omissions and the dots would have been so continual as to worry the reader. This leads me to revert to what I said above. The reader must remember that what is printed in this volume is only a very small portion of the diaries and that the extracts were embedded in a mass of matter unconnected with Virginia Woolf's writing. Unless this is constantly borne in mind, the book will give a very distorted view of her life and her character.

Virginia Woolf does not always indicate in the diary where she is when she is writing it and it is rarely of much importance that the reader should know. The following facts will probably clear up any doubt in any particular case. From 1915 to March, 1924, we lived at Hogarth House, Richmond. This in the diary is often referred to simply as "Hogarth." At the same time we also had a lease of Asheham House, near Lewes, in Sussex, referred to in the diary sim-

180

ply as "Asheham." We used Asheham ordinarily only for
week-ends and holidays. In 1919 the lease of Asheham
House came to an end and we bought Monks House, Rodmell, near Lewes, moving into it in September, 1919. In
1924 we sold Hogarth House, Richmond, and took a lease of
52 Tavistock Square, W. C. 1, often referred to in the diary
as "Tavistock." We lived there from March, 1924, until
August, 1939, when we moved to 37 Mecklenburgh Square,
W. C. 1. In 1940 the house in Mecklenburgh Square was so
badly damaged by bombs that all the furniture had to be removed and we lived until Virginia Woolf's death in 1941 at
Monks House.

I append to this preface a glossary of names of persons used in the diary which will help the reader to understand who is being referred to in any particular passage.

LEONARD WOOLF

1 January, 1953

WILLIAM BUTLER YEATS

John Millington Synge died in 1909, at the age of thirty-eight. In his youth he was enthusiastic about natural history and music, and, after graduating from Trinity College, Dublin, went to Germany to pursue his studies to become a professional violinist. Later he renounced his musical ambitions when he became convinced that writing was his talent. Synge wrote dramas, verse, essays, and other forms of literary prose, but his reputation-- Yeats hailed him as the greatest dramatic genius of Ireland--rests largely on two plays of Irish peasant life: one a comedy in prose but sternly realistic, The Playboy of the Western World; and the other, a stark and uncompromising tragedy, Riders to the Sea.

In the same year that Riders to the Sea was published, Synge finished a three-act play entitled The Well of the Saints which was produced by the Abbey Theatre in February, 1905, and published in book form at that time. In his introduction to the first edition of this play, Yeats tells of discovering Synge in a students' hotel in the Latin Quarter of Paris and advising him, as a would-be writer, to go to the Aran Islands and "live there as if you were one of the people themselves; express a life that has never found expression." Synge followed Yeats' advice, made four trips to the Islands for varying periods of time, and found in the customs, language, and superstitions of the Irish peasants who lived there much that he later recreated in his plays and other writings. One such myth, which may have inspired The Well of the Saints, concerned a miraculous cure for the blind from the waters of

a holy well near the church of St. Carolan. In the
play a blind and ugly couple, Martin and Mary Droul,
are led to believe themselves young and handsome by
the stories which are told to them by the villagers.
A wandering saint brings them the gift of vision and
with it disillusionment. They cannot bear the sight
of one another and they do not find pleasure in the
world in which now they see their villagers live.
When later on they begin to lose their sight again,
they come together and refuse the saint's offer to
restore their sight by another miracle.

The Well of the Saints is a fable and its purpose
is to show the irreconcilability between the dream
world and reality. Yeats points to the moral in his
introduction to the play: "Those two blind people ...
are so transposed by the dream that they choose
blindness rather than reality." In their refusal of
the saint's offer of permanent sight, Martin and
Mary Droul reject what they have briefly encountered
in the all-seeing world of the villagers for the illusions which they experience in blindness. In the current phrase of to-day, it might be said that they prefer doing their own thing. In their blindness they appear to find values which escape the villagers. As
the play ends, one leaves them ugly, apparently disillusioned, and making, one feels, a rueful rather
than a confident decision to depart the village for
regions in the South, where they hope they will be
"hearing a soft wind turning round the little leaves
of the spring and feeling the sun."

The theme of the irreconcilability of the dream
and reality is to be found in other writers since
Synge's play was produced. In The Enchanted Cottage (1922) by Sir Arthur Pinero, a crippled war
veteran marries a rather unattractive old maid in
order to escape the meddlings of his relatives. A
blind friend and neighbor, Major Hillgrove, is led
to believe by the connivance of a servant, who is
thought to have supernatural powers, that the marriage of the veteran and old maid has brought them
strength and beauty, a credulity which they themselves are encouraged to accept by a dream sequence in which they live as the servant described
them to Major Hargrove. When later their relatives
arrive for a visit, they see nothing different about

the two, and the illusion of beauty and grace is dispelled. Although disillusioned, they still feel they have found happiness. Again, a similar theme is to be found in Charlie Chaplin's <u>City Lights</u>. Here a blind girl has her vision restored by the efforts of a tramp. She has always assumed that the man who had made it possible for her to regain her vision was a rich and rather grand person. When she meets and discovers, by the accident of their hands touching, that the awkward, baggy-trousered tramp is her hero, she is disenchanted and the shock of recognition is heart-rending.

PREFACE BY WILLIAM BUTLER YEATS

to J. M. Synge's
<u>The Well of the Saints</u>

Six years ago I was staying in a students' hotel in the Latin Quarter, and somebody, whose name I cannot recollect, introduced me to an Irishman, who, even poorer than myself, had taken a room at the top of the house. It was J. M. Synge, and I, who thought I knew the name of every Irishman who was working at literature, had never heard of him. He was a graduate of Trinity College, Dublin, too, and Trinity College does not, as a rule, produce artistic minds. He told me that he had been living in France and Germany, reading French and German literature, and that he wished to become a writer. He had, however, nothing to show but one or two poems and impressionistic essays, full of that kind of morbidity that has its root in too much brooding over methods of expression, and ways of looking upon life, which come, not out of life, but out of literature, images reflected from mirror to mirror. He had wandered among people whose life is as picturesque as the Middle Ages, playing his fiddle to Italian sailors, and listening to stories in Bavarian woods, but life had cast no light into his writings. He had learned Irish years ago, but had begun to forget it, for the only language that interested him was that conventional language of modern poetry which has begun to make us all weary. I was very weary of it, for I had finished <u>The Secret Rose,</u> and felt how it had separated my imagination from life, sending my Red Hanrahan, who should

have trodden the same roads with myself, into some undis-
coverable country. I said: "Give up Paris. You will never
create anything by reading Racine, and Arthur Symons will
always be a better critic of French literature. Go to the
Aran Islands. Live there as if you were one of the people
themselves; express a life that has never found expression."
I had just come from Aran, and my imagination was full of
those grey islands where men must reap with knives because
of the stones.

He went to Aran and became a part of its life, living
upon salt fish and eggs, talking Irish for the most part, but
listening also to the beautiful English which has grown up in
Irish-speaking districts, and takes its vocabulary from the
time of Malory and of the translators of the Bible, but its
idiom and its vivid metaphor from Irish. When Mr. Synge
began to write in this language, Lady Gregory had already
used it finely in her translations of Dr. Hyde's lyrics and
plays, or of old Irish literature, but she had listened with
different ears. He made his own selection of word and
phrase, choosing what would express his own personality.
Above all, he made word and phrase dance to a very strange
rhythm, which will always, till his plays have created their
own tradition, be difficult to actors who have not learned it
from his lips. It is essential, for it perfectly fits the drifting emotion, the dreaminess, the vague yet measureless desire, for which he would create a dramatic form. It blurs
definition, clear edges, everything that comes from the will,
it turns imagination from all that is of the present, like a
gold background in a religious picture, and it strengthens in
every emotion whatever comes to it from far off, from
brooding memory and dangerous hope. When he brought
The Shadow of the Glen, his first play, to the Irish National
Theatre Society, the players were puzzled by the rhythm,
but gradually they became certain that his Woman of the
Glen, as melancholy as a curlew, driven to distraction by
her own sensitiveness, her own fineness, could not speak
with any other tongue, that all his people would change their
life if the rhythm changed. Perhaps no Irish countryman
had ever that exact rhythm in his voice, but certainly if Mr.
Synge had been born a countryman, he would have spoken
like that. It makes the people of his imagination a little
disembodied; it gives them a kind of innocence even in their
anger and their cursing. It is part of its maker's attitude
towards the world, for while it makes the clash of wills

among his persons indirect and dreamy, it helps him to see
the subject-matter of his art with wise, clear-seeing, unre-
flecting eyes; to preserve the integrity of art in an age of
reasons and purposes. Whether he write of old beggars by
the roadside, lamenting over the misery and ugliness of life,
or of an old Aran woman mourning her drowned sons, or of
a young wife married to an old husband, he has no wish to
change anything, to reform anything; all these people pass by
as before an open window, murmuring strange, exciting
words.

If one has not fine construction, one has not drama,
but if one has not beautiful or powerful and individual speech,
one has not literature, or, at any rate, one has not great
literature. Rabelais, Villon, Shakespeare, William Blake,
would have known one another by their speech. Some of
them knew how to construct a story, but all of them had
abundant, resonant, beautiful, laughing, living speech. It is
only the writers of our modern dramatic movement, our scientific dramatists, our naturalists of the stage, who have
thought it possible to be like the greatest, and yet to cast
aside even the poor persiflage of the comedians, and to write
in the impersonal language that has come, not out of individual life, nor out of life at all, but out of necessities of com-
merce, of Parliament, of Board Schools, of hurried journeys
by rail.

If there are such things as decaying art and decaying
institutions, their decay must begin when the element they
receive into their care from the life of every man in the
world begins to rot. Literature decays when it no longer
makes more beautiful, or more vivid, the language which
unites it to all life, and when one finds the criticism of the
student, and the purpose of the reformer, and the logic of the
man of science, where there should have been the reveries
of the common heart, ennobled into some raving Lear or unabashed Don Quixote. One must not forget that the death of
language, the substitution of phrases as nearly impersonal
as algebra for words and rhythms varying from man to man,
is but a part of the tyranny of impersonal things. I have
been reading through a bundle of German plays, and have
found everywhere a desire, not to express hopes and alarms
common to every man that ever came into the world, but
politics or social passion, a veiled or open propaganda.
Now it is duelling that has need of reproof; now it is the

ideas of an actress, returning from the free life of the stage, that must be contrasted with the prejudice of an old-fashioned town; now it is the hostility of Christianity and Paganism in our own day that is to find an obscure symbol in a bell thrown from its tower by spirits of the wood. I compare the work of these dramatists with the greater plays of their Scandinavian master, and remember that even he, who has made so many clear-drawn characters, has made us no abundant character, no man of genius in whom we could believe, and that in him also, even when it is Emperor and Galilean that are face to face, even the most momentous figures are subordinate to some tendency, to some movement, to some inanimate energy, or to some process of thought whose very logic has changed it into mechanism--always to "something other than human life."

We must not measure a young talent, whether we praise or blame, with that of men who are among the greatest of our time, but we may say of any talent, following out a definition, that it takes up the tradition of great drama as it came from the hands of the Masters who are acknowledged by all time, and turns away from a dramatic movement which, though it has been served by fine talent, has been imposed upon us by science, by artificial life, by a passing order.

When the individual life no longer delights in its own energy, when the body is not made strong and beautiful by the activities of daily life, when men have no delight in decorating the body, one may be certain that one lives in a passing order, amid the inventions of a fading vitality. If Homer were alive to-day, he would only resist, after a deliberate struggle, the temptation to find his subject not in Helen's beauty, that every man has desired, nor in the wisdom and endurance of Odysseus that has been the desire of every woman that has come into the world, but in what somebody would describe, perhaps, as "the inevitable contest," arising out of economic causes, between the country-places and small towns on the one hand, and, upon the other, the great city of Troy, representing one knows not what "tendency to centralisation."

Mr. Synge has in common with the great theatre of the world, with that of Greece and that of India, with the creator of Falstaff, with Racine, a delight in language, a preoccupation with individual life. He resembles them also

by a preoccupation with what is lasting and noble, that came
to him, not, as I think, from books, but while he listened to
old stories in the cottages, and contrasted what they remembered with reality. The only literature of the Irish country-
people is their songs, full often of extravagant love, and their
stories of kings and of kings' children. "I will cry my fill,
but not for God, but because Finn and the Fianna are not
living," says Oisin in the story. Every writer, even every
small writer, who has belonged to the great tradition, has
had his dream of an impossibly noble life, and the greater
he is, the more does it seem to plunge him into some beautiful or bitter reverie. Some, and of these are all the earliest poets of the world, gave it direct expression; others min-
gle it so subtly with reality that it is a day's work to disen-
tangle it; others bring it near by showing us whatever is
most its contrary. Mr. Synge, indeed, sets before us ugly,
deformed or sinful people, but his people, moved by no
practical ambition, are driven by a dream of that impossible
life. That we may feel how intensely his Woman of the Glen
dreams of days that shall be entirely alive, she that is "a
hard woman to please" must spend her days between a sour-
faced old husband, a man who goes mad upon the hills, a
craven lad and a drunken tramp; and those two blind people
of The Well of the Saints are so transformed by the dream
that they choose blindness rather than reality. He tells us
of realities, but he knows that art has never taken more
than its symbols from anything that the eye can see or the
hand measure.

It is the preoccupation of his characters with their
dream that gives his plays their drifting movement, their
emotional subtlety. In most of the dramatic writing of our
time, and this is one of the reasons why our dramatists do
not find the need for a better speech, one finds a simple motive lifted, as it were, into the full light of the stage. The
ordinary student of drama will not find anywhere in The Well
of the Saints that excitement of the will in the presence of
attainable advantages, which he is accustomed to think the
natural stuff of drama, and if he see it played he will wonder why act is knitted to act so loosely, why it is all like
a decoration on a flat surface, why there is so much leisure
in the dialogue, even in the midst of passion. If he see The
Shadow of the Glen, he will ask, Why does this woman go out
of her house? Is it because she cannot help herself, or is
she content to go? Why is it not all made clearer? And

yet, like everybody when caught up into great events, she does many things without being quite certain why she does them. She hardly understands at moments why her action has a certain form, more clearly than why her body is tall or short, fair or brown. She feels an emotion that she does not understand. She is driven by desires that need for their expression, not "I admire this man," or "I must go, whether I will or no," but words full of suggestion, rhythms of voice, movements that escape analysis. In addition to all this, she had something that she shares with none but the children of one man's imagination. She is intoxicated by a dream which is hardly understood by herself, but possesses her like something half remembered on a sudden wakening.

While I write, we are rehearsing The Well of the Saints, and are painting for it decorative scenery, mountains in one or two flat colours and without detail, ashtrees and red salleys with something of recurring pattern in their woven boughs. For though the people of the play use no phrase they could not use in daily life, we know that we are seeking to express what no eye has ever seen.

ABBEY THEATRE
January 27, 1905

ACKNOWLEDGMENTS

Acknowledgments are due individual publishers and copyright holders (or their representatives) for permission to reprint as follows:

"Introduction by W. H. Auden for the British edition of THE ART OF EATING by Faber Ltd from the British edition of THE ART OF EATING by M. F. K. Fisher © W. H. Auden 1963."

"Introduction by Stanley Baldwin (p. ix-xii). From Precious Bane by Mary Webb. Introduction by the Rt. Hon. Stanley Baldwin. Published in the United States, © 1926, 1929, by E. P. Dutton & Co., Inc., and reprinted with their permission."

"Introduction by James M. Barrie (p. v-xi). From Conrad in Quest of His Youth by Leonard Merrick. Copyright, 1919 by E. P. Dutton & Co., Inc.; renewal, copyright, 1946 by Lesley Merrick. Reprinted by permission of the publishers, E. P. Dutton & Co., Inc."

"Biographical introduction by Edmund Blunden to John Clare: Poems from Manuscript by John Clare. London, Cobden-Sanderson, 1920. Reprinted by permission of A D Peters & Co Ltd."

"Introduction by Elmer Davis to This Is London by Edward Murrow. Copyright © 1941 by Edward R. Murrow; renewed 1969 by Janet Murrow and Charles Murrow. Reprinted by permission of Simon & Schuster, Inc."

"Foreword by Ira Dilworth. From Klee Wyck by Emily Carr. Toronto, Clarke, Irwin & Company Limited, copyright 1941, Centennial ed. 1971. Reprinted by permission of Clarke, Irwin & Company Limited."

191

ACKNOWLEDGMENTS

"'Andy Adams, Cowboy Chronicler,' by J. Frank Dobie. From the SOUTHWEST Review vol II, No. 2, January, 1926. Copyright 1926 by the SOUTHWEST Review. Reprinted by permission of the Southern Methodist University Press."

"'Notes on Lord of the Flies' by E. L. Epstein. From the Capricorn edition of Lord of the Flies by William Golding. New York, Capricorn Books, 1954. Reprinted by permission of Coward, McCann & Geoghegan, Inc."

"Foreword by Morris L. Ernst. From Ulysses by James Joyce, with a foreword by Morris L. Ernst and the decision of the U. S. District Court rendered by John M. Woolsey. New York, The Modern Library, © 1946. Reprinted by permission of Random House, Inc."

"Introductory note by E. M. Forster. From Twenty Years A-growing by Maurice O'Sullivan. London, Chatto & Windus Ltd., 1933. Reprinted by permission of Chatto & Windus Ltd and the E. M. Forster's literary estate."

"Preface by Sigmund Freud. Reprinted with the permission of Farrar, Straus & Giroux, Inc. from RITUAL by Theodor Reik, Preface by Sigmund Freud, tr. from 2d German ed. by Douglas Bryan. Copyright 1946 by Theodor Reik, copyright renewed 1974 by Arthur Reik."

"Preface by John F. Kennedy to LOOKING OUTWARD: YEARS OF CRISIS AT THE UNITED NATIONS by Adlai Stevenson, Edited by Robert L. and Selma Schiffer. Copyright © 1963 by Adlai Stevenson and Selma Schiffer. Reprinted by permission of Harper & Row, Publishers, Inc."

"Introduction by James D. McCallum. From Java Head by Joseph Hergesheimer. N.Y., Alfred A. Knopf, 1929 © (1919, 1926). Reprinted by permission of Random House, Inc."

"'A Memorial Tribute to Carl Sandburg' by Archibald MacLeish. From The Massachusetts Review 9 (Winter, 1960) 41-44. Reprinted by permission of The Massachusetts Review, Inc."

"Foreword by Paul C. Mangelsdorf. Reprinted by

ACKNOWLEDGMENTS

permission of the author and publishers from EXPERIMENTS IN PLANT HYBRIDISATION by Gregor Mendel, with Foreword by Paul C. Mangelsdorf, Cambridge, Massachusetts: Harvard University Press, © 1965 by the President and Fellows of Harvard College."

"From DISTRESSING DIALOGUES, Harper & Row. Copyright 1924, 1951, by Edna St. Vincent Millay and Norma Millay Ellis."

"Introduction by Christopher Morley. From <u>Nine Answers</u> by G. Bernard Shaw. Privately Printed for Jerome Kern, 1923. Reprinted with the kind permission of Mrs. Blythe Morley Brennan."

"Foreword by Allan Nevins. From pp. ix-xvi 'Foreword' by Allan Nevins in PROFILES IN COURAGE, Inaugural Edition by John F. Kennedy. Copyright © 1961 by John F. Kennedy. Reprinted by permission of Harper & Row, Publishers, Inc."

"'Stephen Crane: An Estimate' by Vincent Starrett. From <u>Men, Women and Boats</u> ed. with an introd. by Vincent Starrett. New York, Boni & Liveright, copyright 1921. (Modern Library of the World's Best Books). Reprinted by permission of Random House, Inc."

"Foreword by Walter Prescott Webb. From <u>Texas County Histories: A Bibliography</u> by H. Bailey Carroll. Austin, Texas State Historical Association, 1943. Reprinted by permission of the Texas State Historical Association."

"Foreword by Edward Weeks. From <u>Good-bye, Mr. Chips</u> by James Hilton. An Atlantic Monthly Press Book: Little, Brown and Company, copyright © 1962 by Alice Hilton. Reprinted by permission of Little, Brown and Company, Publishers."

"Introduction by Eudora Welty. From <u>Hanging by a Thread</u> edited by Joan Kahn. Boston, Houghton Mifflin Company, 1969, copyright © by Eudora Welty. Reprinted by permission of Russell & Volkening, Inc. as Agents for the Author."

"Introduction by Edmund Wilson from The Sun Rise

ACKNOWLEDGMENTS

Edition, vol. 1 of IN OUR TIME by Ernest Hemingway is reprinted by permission of Charles Scribner's Sons. Copyright 1925, 1930 Charles Scribner's Sons."

"Preface by Leonard Woolf. From A WRITER'S DIARY by Virginia Woolf, edited by Leonard Woolf. New York, Harcourt, Brace and Company. Copyright 1953, 1954, by Leonard Woolf. Reprinted by permission of Harcourt Brace Jovanovich, Inc."

"Preface by William Butler Yeats to the first edition of The Well of the Saints by J. M. Synge. Reprinted from ESSAYS AND INTRODUCTIONS by William Butler Yeats. New York, Macmillan Publishing Co., 1961. Copyright © by Mrs. W. B. Yeats, 1961. Reprinted by permission of the Macmillan Publishing Co., Inc."